# Acknowledgements

Thanks to all my English teaching colleagues at Park College, Eastbourne, for many years of putting up with the noise from my classroom next door, for making me laugh, and for teaching me everything I know about the long novel. Thanks also to ten years of fantastic Park College students, who gave everything a go with such gusto. Thanks also to Anne Fairhall and the NATE editorial team, and to Siobhain Archer, Alison Smith, Katie Green and Garry Pratt of Teachit, for all their wise feedback on the drafts, impeccable good taste, and generous support when I turned into the GCSE-retake-student-from-hell in the redrafting.

This book is dedicated to my friend Andrew Moore, who didn't live to see it written, but without whose encouragement to take risks it would never have been started.

# The Full English

## An A-Z handbook of English teaching activities

## Julie Blake

**NATE**

teachit.co.uk
ENGLISH TEACHING ONLINE

Published by the **National Association for the Teaching of English (NATE)**, the UK subject association for all aspects of English from pre-school to university. The association aims to support effective teaching and learning, to keep teachers informed about current developments and to provide them with a national voice.

*The Full English* has been published in close association with **Teachit:** English teaching online. **www.teachit.co.uk** is an education resource used by thousands of teachers nationwide. The Teachit libraries offer thousands of pages of classroom materials and interactive activities all created by working teachers. Teachit shares a proportion of its revenues with the teachers who contribute materials.

© Julie Blake, 2006

ISBN  978 1 90470 920 6

First published 2006
Reprinted 2007

See *The Full English* website at **www.fullenglish.co.uk**

**British Library Cataloguing in Publication data**
A catalogue record for this book is available from the British Library.

NATE
50 Broadfield Road
Sheffield
S8 OXJ
T: 0114 2555419  F: 0114 2555296
E: info@nate.org.uk
**www.nate.org.uk**

Printed and bound in Europe by the Alden Group, Oxford

# Contents

# Introduction

This book started a long time ago. As a PGCE student desperate for teaching ideas, I hoarded anything I could lay my hands on. I squinted at the sheet my mentor gave me, called '20 things to do with a book', a side of A4 that had been re-photocopied so many times on machines barely out of the Banda era that it was almost illegible. I squandered my grant ('Banda machines, student grants – how old is this woman?!') photocopying (legitimate) chunks of a very good series of books about teaching English that I have only ever been able to describe since as 'yellow'. And when I got my first teaching post, I collected a blue cardboard folder from the stationery cupboard and put all my scraggy old bits of paper in it.

Of course, in your first year of teaching you're supposed to die of the shock, so I didn't add much to the blue folder then, but at the end of it I moved elsewhere for a permanent contract and the head of department handed me a comb-bound compilation of teaching ideas. Into the blue folder it went. And back out of the blue folder came all kinds of experiments as I systematically worked my way through every single technique in there. One by one. Throwing out my teaching materials at the end of every academic year in order to make way for more experiments. No-one ever told me that was really weird, freaky behaviour…

Somewhere along the way, I saw a repeat of the movie *Working Girl*. Sure, I'm always a sucker for a girl-from-the-wrong-side-of-the-tracks-hits-the-big-time story, but what distracted me from my marking pile was the scene where Harrison Ford asks Melanie Griffiths where she gets all her ideas from. She tells him she reads all kinds of stuff all the time, not just the hot shot business journals, and, finding ideas everywhere, she cuts them out and keeps them while she thinks about them. 'Yes, yes, yes, yes!' I exploded in a Molly Bloom moment all of my own, 'That's what I do!' Except I hadn't been doing the cutting and kept getting annoyed that I couldn't remember the ideas I'd come across.

After that, no newspaper, magazine or random act of information was safe. Anyone visiting who idly picked up the paper would have the novel experience of it dissolving into hamster bedding in their hands. But the blue folder grew. I started adding in little notes on the backs of envelopes of things I'd seen other teachers doing, and handouts from all kinds of odd INSET sessions, and little features from The *Guardian* that I thought might work as writing activities. Reader, I was a techniques junkie.

But mostly I kept the blue folder going because I'm rubbish at remembering stuff. I would try something out, find out its strengths and limitations, then do something different the next time and forget all about it. I needed the folder in order to keep coming back and refreshing my ideas, trying things out again, or in different combinations.

Eventually I got involved in mentoring new teachers. By this stage the blue folder had been shoved down the back of countless filing cabinets only to be retrieved, dog-eared and coffee-stained, at the start of each new academic year. But to each new ITT or NQT I would hand over the battered blue folder in a preposterously ceremonial fashion, offering all my worldly wisdom like some wizened old hag-mentor in an epic fantasy, and threatening strange curses on their fertility if it didn't come back to me. Somehow it always did, though that may have had something to do with sensible revulsion at the nastiness of the yellowing papers inside. And every time it did I muttered apologetically, 'One day I'll write it all down properly.'

I never did. And then Siân pitched up, a shiny young NQT on our team of old lags. By now the blue folder was really quite foul, and anyway it was never anything more than a random collection of clippings and copies. I wasn't mentoring Siân, but she observed me teach many times and eventually reached the limits of her frustration, exploding, with entirely good cause, 'Will you stop telling me it's easy and explain what you're doing!' Well, that's the polite version – if memory serves me correctly, there may also have been a few eye-melting Welsh expletives in there...

But there was a merger and a restructuring and, well, you know how it goes... So, instead of finding the time to give that kind of detailed explanation, I tried to buy Siân a book. Hours spent trying to track down the one that would do the job were fruitless. Of course there are plenty of more or less useful books, but I didn't want to give advice about educational strategies and assessment objectives, generalised tips, generic teaching ideas for any subject, or text-specific photocopiable worksheets. I wanted something that would explain a technique, that would show how to apply it to specific texts or tasks but be transferable to others, and that would be clear in the pedagogical principles underpinning it. I also wanted it to show how much fun can be had in teaching English.

So, I wrote it myself. Too late. Siân left the teaching profession. But here it is, for everyone who knows that feeling of frustration, who wants some new ideas, or some new ways of looking at old ideas. The ideas are not mine. Like a Victorian butterfly collector, I have rounded them up, sorted them according to their underlying principles, and explained them. This is the collective body of knowledge that we all share, and it's a work in progress. There will of course be techniques that I haven't come across, and the applications described here can only give an indicative flavour of how they might be used. We all teach in different ways and in different contexts. What works here won't necessarily work there. That's what makes teaching fun.

The title *The Full English* should not be taken literally – it's a playful title that has more to do with my love of bacon and eggs than anything else; it is not the full picture, nor can it be in a profession of wonderfully creative and inventive people. But I hope the techniques described here will inspire teachers to try a few new things out, to play around a little (or a lot) with texts and tasks, to have enough confidence in the pedagogical underpinning to give creative activities a go, and to have as much fun teaching as I've had so far.

And Siân, get yourself back into a classroom. It's never too late.

# Actioning

## Movements and gestures to fit the words

## The basic idea

Take a speech or scene, any speech or scene. Divide it into sensible units of meaning according to the text – phrases, lines, small blocks of lines. Students explore the emotion of the speech or scene, finding a movement or gesture to go with each chunk of words. Keep focus on expression of emotion, not dumb-show replication of the business of the text. Prepare in small groups or do spontaneously in whole class act-in. Explore issues and ideas arising.

## Applying it

- Try it with any powerplay soliloquy you like, but it's also good with exchanges between characters who are trying to keep their cards a bit closer to their chests. Try it with Duke Orsino and Viola in Act 2 Scene 4 of *Twelfth Night*. For a great variety of short extracts that might lead into all sorts of other creative or critical things when you're not chained to the set text, check out Jones and Marlow's *Duologues for all Accents and Ages* and their *More Duologues*.

- Works with poems too, bringing a sense of the oral tradition of poetry as well as focusing minds on mood and voice. As good with Shakespeare's sonnets as with modern performance poetry. For a poem of the month by a contemporary performance poet, check out 'Apples and Snakes' at **www.applesandsnakes.org.**

- Charles Dickens was by all accounts a masterly reader of his own work, using his voice, as well as movement and gesture to wow the audience in sell out shows. Why not try it with prose too? Gets students feeling the texture of the writer's style which can be harder to do with prose than other more obviously crafted forms.

## What's the point?

To encourage close reading of the text and precise thinking about the emotion swirling about, between and beneath the lines. Insisting on one action or movement to go with each line can make for more dynamic and engaged reading or performance. This is especially true with groups or individuals who are dramatically challenged as making a single movement or gesture is not too intimidating. For students who like to move about and/or have good physical intelligence, this activity can be a joy. Just bear in mind that not all kinaesthetic learners enjoy acting...

### Tricks of the trade

Try doing it all together first to build confidence and reduce inhibition. Get students in a circle. Divide the units of meaning between them, going round the circle. Give them a minute to try out a few moves, then have a class action reading. Explore what happened, what connections there were between their movements, how it could be developed, and have another go. Then they might have the hang of it for further scenes or speeches to be worked on more independently.

### Variations on a theme

- A popular variation is to walk as the words are said, changing pace and/or direction at each punctuation mark. This shows bodily how broken or how fluid the speech is. Vary further by introducing pauses to reflect stronger punctuation.

- Use ideas developed in the actioning workshop to help write a set of director's notes for the scene.

# Adaptations
## Long live the BBC and/or Merchant Ivory

## The basic idea

The film of the book, the short story of the poem, the play of the song, the modern prose version of the old play, the outer space musical version, the adaptation for young children, the graded reader version for language learners. Write it. Or with existing adaptations, read it or watch it. Compare and contrast. Key scenes from several adaptations make for good exploration of alternative interpretations.

### Applying it

• Compare the portrayal of whatever you fancy in any two or three film adaptations of the play. For a timeless classic, take a close look at the fight scenes in *Romeo and Juliet* by Baz Luhrmann (1997) and Franco Zeffirelli (1968). See Teachit's resource at **Key Stage 3/4>Drama>Romeo and Juliet>Compare two film versions of Romeo and Juliet**. The 2001 made-for-TV *Othello*, starring Christopher Eccleston, is a cracking example of a modern adaptation which could be contrasted well with any standard version.

• Need help finding adaptations? Check out the Internet Movie Database at **www.imdb.com**. Wikipedia also useful at **www.wikipedia.com**: check out their *Hamlet* page for details of some of the 22 movie versions, a fascinating range of popular culture references and adaptations (did you know there was a *The Simpsons* version?!), and songs.

• 'It's not as good as the book' but always interesting to see what's been done to transform a novel for the silver screen. Check out Teachit's **Key Stage 3>Prose>Great Expectations by Charles Dickens>Resource 7** for detailed notes on David Lean's 1944 version and the BBC's 1999 version.

• Compare the spoof and the original as in Teachit's **Key Stage 4>Media & Non-Fiction>Without A Clue> Essay guide**. Invites comparison with a more traditional version of any Sherlock Holmes made-for-TV and, of course, the original story. Nice...

• But it's not all about watching telly. A former colleague's favourite activity in the whole world: *Wuthering Heights*, Emily Bronte Vs Kate Bush's No 1 hit Vs Hermann's opera Vs Cliff Richard's musical. Cool... Well, maybe not the last one there...

### What's the point?

It invites comparative thinking, the development and/or critique of alternative interpretations, and can lead the way to interesting discussion about the role and function of adaptations, er, and of literature's place in society if you want to get really deep... You only have to look at Andrew Davies to see how highly a talent for literary adaptation is valued by the cultural bastion of the BBC. There's even a whole Oscar for best adaptation, so get them going, but make sure they are very clear that you are to be acknowledged in their acceptance speech.

### Tricks of the trade

Usual tricks about watching telly in class: don't expect much insightful critical reaction to a solid chunk of an hour's viewing on a small screen sitting on hard seats. Projection onto the big screen makes it a more absorbing cinematic experience, but otherwise it can be better to watch it in shorter sections, even just key scenes. See **Zombie killers** (page 150) for more ideas on tackling this.

If writing adaptations, explore what a screenplay looks like first. Emma Thompson has helpfully published both screenplay and filming diary for *Sense and Sensibility*.

Allow students space to exercise the full scope of their creativity in this activity. Their version may be bonkers, but it may also be brilliant, and as long as they can justify it and evaluate its success, they will have learned a great deal. After all, what English teacher would have thought *Cats* was a good idea?...

**Variations on a theme**

- Get students producing their own adaptations of the set text, or key parts of it, in whatever genre they like: film, drama, song, write the novel of the drama (as with *Dr Who* novels, and *Buffy The Vampire Slayer* novels), comic book - the possibilities are vast...

- Give students the opportunity, if you can, to write an adaptation of any book they want to. A colleague's work with one group of students culminated in a tour of French primary schools with a singalong version of everyone's favourite children's book, *The Hungry Caterpillar*...

**Whizzing it**

With some PCs or laptops and digital clips of the scenes you're working on, small groups of students can be watching and working on different scenes, with far greater interactivity as they pause and replay and discuss as they go. Also great opportunities to watch on the IWB and use all the note-making features as you pause and discuss.

# Additions & omissions

Bits in and out of alternative editions

## The basic idea

Some texts exist in different versions, such as the different folio editions of Shakespeare plays, or the expurgated and unexpurgated editions of Anne Frank's diary. Get your hands on these, or at least on some of the 'missing' bits. Get students exploring the similarities and differences, the reasons why the bits were included or excluded, and whether they would have made the same editorial judgements either then or now.

### Applying it

• Compare the 'To be or not to be' soliloquy from *Hamlet* from the first quarto with the one we accept as the standard edition. It starts like this:

> *To be, or not to be, I there's the point,*
>
> *To Die, to sleepe, is that all? I all:*
>
> *No, to sleepe, to dreame, I mary there it goes,*
>
> *For in that dreame of death, when wee awake,*
>
> *And borne before an everlasting Judge,*
>
> *From whence no passenger ever retur'nd,*
>
> *The undiscovered country, at whose sight*
>
> *The happy smile, and the accursed damn'd.*

• Check out the New York Times article about the controversy over the missing pages of *The Diary of Anne Frank* at **www.annefrank.org> News>Web dossier>disclosure 1998**.

• Look at children's editions of classic texts such as *Robinson Crusoe* or *Gulliver's Travels* to explore what has been included, omitted or bowdlerised.

### What's the point?

It encourages students to see books as the product of decisions made by both writers and editors. This throws small but useful hand grenades at the idea of the divinely ordained text, opens up new lines of enquiry and interpretation, and can inspire students who are intrigued by the whole heady world of publishing. With something like the Anne Frank, it can stimulate lively discussion about censorship, freedom of expression and institutional control of literature; with the Shakespeare, questions about directorial decision-making; with both, interesting questions about authenticity and literary merit.

### Tricks of the trade

Good questioning is needed to draw out the critical issues otherwise students can make reductive judgements based on which edition they have actually been given as their set text! Comparing the complete texts would be time consuming and tedious: best to work with short tasty extracts. With the Anne Frank, either rugby tackle your resident conspiracy theorists into a tight stranglehold, or tackle the issue head on for a very lively little unit of work.

### Variations on a theme

• Role play director and actor arguing for and against the inclusion of the extra or alternative dialogue.

• Write different reviews based on interpretations of the different text editions.

# Anthologies

Creating ones worth reading...

## The basic idea

Students have a pile of stuff: poems, short stories, magazine features of all kinds, variety of literary and non-literary texts on a common theme. Written by themselves, other students, amateur or professional writers, local or global, previously published or not yet published. They work together to decide which texts should be included in a specified anthology of work.

### Applying it

• Create an anthology of favourite poems, to introduce the study of poetry at any level. Send a copy to feeder schools as a link activity. For a very neat set of task instructions that could be used with any age/stage see Teachit's **Key Stage 3>Poetry>An introduction to poetry>Creating an anthology**.

•Create a thematic anthology as a pre-reading task for a related text.

• From a large anthology prescribed for study, create a mini-anthology; from a small anthology prescribed for study, create a maxi-anthology.

• For media work, compile clips of the ten best-ever films, soaps, cop shows, comedies, cartoons, or whatever, and have students justify their choices to a panel. Think Channel 4 Saturday night filler TV.

• For A2 Literature, or A2 Language & Literature, have students creating synoptic anthologies of their own devising on specific themes or genres.

### What's the point?

It is good for the development of decision making and aesthetic judge-ment. Students have to think carefully about what criteria they are going to use for inclusion in the anthology, debate their application of those criteria, and work together to reach a consensus. These are high level skills, underpinned by in-built wider reading and independent exploration of texts.

### Tricks of the trade

If you want students to find texts, you need to make sure they know where and how to look or it can become a bit of a smash and grab job. Work with the librarian to help develop these, building as rich a variety of pathways as you can. Also spend time working with students to understand what a rich and rewarding anthology is like, and what selection criteria might underpin this, as their experience is often of the random pick'n'mix variety.

### Variations on a theme

• Create an anthology of original writing by students: 'best in class', get older students anthologising younger students' work, run a competition in which your students are the judges. This may work best as an enrichment activity.

• When the prescribed anthology is dreary, loathed by you and your students, set them the task of improving it and writing to the publisher with their recommendations. Deep joy…

• Give interested students free rein within the general parameters of the task; less interested students can work from a given pile of stuff.

### Whizzing it

Use Teachit's splendid Poem template in **Whizzythings>Publisher**. And/or get your students producing multimedia anthologies with images and audio files of existing or created readings of the poems.

# Archaeological dig

Discover culture/society from the fragments shored against our ruins

## The basic idea

Give students a lucky bag of artefacts from a particular culture or society or period or story. They sift through these, trying to determine what kind of people created them, what kinds of interests they had, their values and attitudes to the world, the connections and stories that might hold them together. Use to explore cultural context of a text, or to stimulate creative writing in a particular period or imaginative setting.

## Applying it

- Explore the roots of the English language and the kinds of people who brought their words with them, with Teachit's **Language library> Language change>A linguistic archaeological dig**.

- Use artefacts or facsimiles to explore the context of soldiers fighting in World War 1. Try the Imperial War Museum's collections online, **www.iwmcollections.org.uk**.

- See the teacher section of the 'Texts in Context' website for several examples of artefact work leading to all sorts of interesting outcomes in English at Key Stages 3 and 5, at **http://bllearning.co.uk/live/ text/teachers/**.

- Try doing it as a pre-reading activity. For 'The Adventure of the Speckled Band', have a clock, a black veil, a return ticket, a tiara, (maybe the cheetah, the baboon and the snake might be a bit tricky…), a cigar, a shawl, brandy, a matchbox, a lamp, black lace, a hunting crop, a poker, a revolver, a cane, and a pipe. What kind of world is evoked? What kind of story is suggested?

## What's the point?

It encourages lots of speculation, careful piecing together of evidence, testing the logic and credibility of each other's ideas, and processes of deduction. It can enable students to discover a cultural context, generally a more joyful process than simply being told about it, and certainly one that encourages greater independence of thought. It can encourage rich and imaginative storytelling.

### Tricks of the trade

Have challenging, quirky and interesting cultural fragments that will snag on the students' imaginations. Make sure there are points of connection between them so it's not just a random pick'n'mix that little coherent sense can be made of. More items and an opportunity to browse between them makes the task easier than fewer, as ideas and connections start to build more quickly.

### Variations on a theme

- Get your local museum education staff involved in a creative writing project, either by bringing artefacts into school or college, or by hosting a workshop at the museum. Some museums have boxes or bags of artefacts that they loan out to schools – don't let the History team have all the fun…

- Give students different selections of objects to mix it up. A big opportunity to differentiate by learning style preference with handling of objects, listening to recordings, reading images and texts.

### Whizzing it

Take digital photos of the objects. Get students slotting them into storyboards in the order they want them to occur in their story, then using this as a writing frame.

# Art attack

Pictures as stimulus for writing

## The basic idea

Get a big box of art postcards. People. Places. Pictures that tell a story. Abstracts that evoke moods. Invite students to select one they like. Crank up the thinking, talking and speculating about the images, and then unleash imaginative writing.

### Applying it

• Use the 26 A-Z paintings Quentin Blake selected for the National Gallery exhibition to stimulate children's creative storytelling, *Tell Me A Picture*. Available in book form with the same title.

• Use pictures as the basis for snapshot haikus.

• Select interesting portraits and write *Talking Heads* style dramatic monologues. Use the 'search the collection' function on the National Portrait Gallery website **www.npg.org.uk** to find thematically related images.

• Use as a pre-reading activity to encourage imaginative engagement with a period, or type of character, or setting. Try the National Portrait Gallery's collection of Regency women portraits before starting *Jane Eyre*. Or their First World War men. Very nice opportunity for creative stimulus.

### What's the point?

Reading images is a valuable activity in its own right, encouraging attention to detail and careful consideration of meanings and attitudes. It creates a space in which imaginative minds can wander, and a richer starting point for storytelling than a blank sheet of paper.

### Tricks of the trade

Choose images your students will find engaging. Ones with a strong sense of narrative are easier to connect with for storytelling, but abstract images can be more provocative for lyrical poetry writing. Have multiple copies of each image available (or make them available in unlimited digital form) so no time or blood gets spilled negotiating who gets what.

### Variations on a theme

• Get larger prints of the images and get students curating their own exhibition of paintings and stories. Great for the showcase corridor and/or another award-winning display for open evening.

• Do it live in an art gallery. Many will have an education team who will do all the work for you while you go to the café/gift shop (well, okay, so maybe that's a bit of a fantasy but they do run workshops).

• Get the students to do the preparation for you. Show them a gallery website and how to search the collection. Their homework task: to select three images they think would form a good basis for story telling, poetry writing, monologue or whatever. They print them off, bring them in.

### Whizzing it

Show students how to develop a story from an image using the IWB. Whack a copy of the image up in its full digital glory. Annotate with students' ideas and observations, draw together as a collaborative story outline. Then over to them with their chosen image.

# Balloon debate

Get rid of the dross

## The basic idea

Each student is one character. The characters are in a plummeting hot air balloon (or a stricken life raft) and some of them have got to be thrown overboard for the rest to survive. They must decide who is going to make this sacrifice for the greater good. Result: raging debate about each character's virtues and vices, a lot of laughing, and when a character's back is up against the basket, some really interesting arguments about subtle details and ambiguities. That's what I call a result.

## Applying it

• Works a treat with the pilgrims from the *General Prologue to the Canterbury Tales*, though at least one student will always point out that hot air balloons hadn't actually been invented then.

• Give it a go with Phillip Pullman's *Northern Lights* – lots of characters and some very tricky decisions to be made there.

• Instead of characters, give each student responsibility for a poem or text from an anthology. Their job is to defend its inclusion, which can challenge them to find positive qualities in texts they have previously found tedious. Alternatively, it can be very cathartic as students gleefully throw their texts overboard at the first opportunity…

## What's the point?

It gets discussion going immediately and everyone has to join in at some point (unless they're a complete refusenik). Students have to think hard about all the details of their character, select the most useful, and think on their feet in response to the argument and counterargument of others. As it develops, students often start to develop unholy alliances with other characters in order to save their skin, then there are betrayals when the crunch comes, and all this is rich material for post-activity discussion and/or creative writing. It gives students a valuable opportunity to engage creatively with the characters of a text.

### Tricks of the trade

A bizarre combination of good classroom management and a healthy respect for creative unpredictability is the best way on this one. Start by deciding how to get students to prepare for their role. You might do this after you've studied the text, as a kind of rounding off exercise, in which case not much prep is needed. It works well before this stage too, and even as a pre-reading activity, but for this you need to give appropriate preparation time and resources.

To keep a fairly tight rein on the proceedings, do it in small groups: have only a few key characters in the basket, or give students multiple 'lives' to play with so that once one of their characters is out they can be reincarnated as another one. Then compare who survived and why. Everyone participates and it's just a more imaginative variation of regular small group discussion.

For a bigger challenge, doing it with bigger groups (even whole class with smaller set sizes or more mature students) creates a more dramatic sense of occasion – a real classroom happening - but you may have to give a role to those who are thrown overboard early to avoid mischief. Try giving them

an observation role, or play in tag teams, allowing them to tap a character on the shoulder and take his/her place if they've got a good argument.

Decide also how many survivors can stay in the balloon. For ultra-competitive, super-sharp debate, only one can stay. This can get a bit tedious at the end - 'you', 'no you' – and usually argument is ended by one character abandoning the will to live and jumping overboard. Set two survivors and you avoid this, though then students will often try and pick a male and a female so the gender dynamics get twisted up – avoid this by making it clear at the start that this isn't Noah's ark and the future of humanity doesn't depend upon their choice. If you have a lot of delicate little souls who will cry if they get thrown out of the balloon either (a) don't do this activity or (b) increase the number of survivors, say half or two thirds of the group size.

Advance preparation can be a very useful homework task, and can be delicious evil teacher's revenge as students who don't do it often get stuffed in the debate (make sure you point that out to them afterwards, teehee). When the laziest student performs brilliantly regardless, don't get mad, get him/her on the gifted and talented register.

### Variations on a theme

• This is a great activity for effective differentiation as you can determine who gets to be which character. Give students with strong argumentative skills and/or a powerful competitive streak characters whose survival is harder to justify. In the preparation, some students will focus on character detail and straightforward argument; others might be encouraged to think about character connections and counterargument.

• It's also great for giving students a chance to play out different roles in the classroom dynamic. Give over-cosy friendship groups characters who don't see eye to eye; give the disaffected boys heroic character roles and make the girly swots be villains. You never know, it might have interesting results.

• Follow it up with creative writing or drama work based on this scenario, developing the most interesting arguments and ideas, bonds and betrayals into a controlled piece of imaginative work. Nice…

# Betting

Only fake ££, obviously...

## The basic idea

Students have a question and/or a text of some sort and a series of possible answers. They also have a stash of fake money. They have to decide which answer is correct and then they get an opportunity to bet according to their degree of confidence. The idea is to end the session with as much cash as possible. Play as many rounds as you like, individually, in pairs, or any size group you like. Get printable fake money here: **www.moneyinstructor.com >kids and money resources> kids play money**. It's American dollars but at least that way you won't have an angry canteen manager coming at you with a meat cleaver...

### Applying it

- Works really well to focus on matters of written accuracy: give short texts in each round on which students make decisions about spelling, punctuation and grammar.

- Livens up any multiple choice quiz on any topic or text.

- To get them thinking about how openings contain the seeds of endings, give them rounds in which they have excerpts of the openings of novels and a series of short descriptions of possible endings. They read, explore textual evidence carefully, and bet on which endings they think are most likely. Pay out handsomely to the winners and channel the 'no way!' outrage into lively discussion.

- Do it in *Who Wants To Be A Millionaire* format. Same basic idea... Check out Teachit's **Key Stage 3>Drama> Twelfth Night Act 3 Scene 4>Work book 3**.

### What's the point?

Apart from the fact that all your hustlers will immediately come to life in your lesson, it can encourage students to commit to a particular answer. When money (however fake) is at stake, you suddenly get a real seriousness of intent in the classroom. You can feel brains humming in the desire to get it absolutely right. But it's also a smarter technique than that, because if the questions are hard enough, it makes students take risks with their answers, and trust their intuition, and these are valuable exam performance strategies.

### Tricks of the trade

Have it clear in your head how the gambling thing is going to work so that you can explain the rules clearly at the start of the activity. Always best to have a practice round so everyone can see how it works, especially those who aren't good with verbal instruction. Sustain interest by having questions with different degrees of difficulty and complexity. And let the class clean out the bank from time to time – it's good for confidence when the students win, even if you know you just hid some of the money. Er, and obviously don't use this technique if you think the management or parents will object.

### Variations on a theme

- Stretch the strongest students by making sure your questions progress to higher levels in later rounds and/or having 'fiendish' rounds where different stakes apply.

### Whizzing it

Have the questions and answers up on the big screen in powerpoint and animate the correct answer so you look like Chris Tarrant.

# Bingo

Eyes down

## The basic idea

You pick a selection of twenty or thirty key words that you want students to pay attention to. Either by hand, or by free online magic that only takes 17.37 seconds, create a set of bingo cards, each featuring a random selection from this pool of key words. Play the game in one of many different ways. Lines, bonus squares and full houses all win prizes and/or glory. Online bingo card magic available at **www.teach-nology.com> Worksheets>Bingo card generator**.

### Applying it

- Terminology test: pull a definition out of the bag, call it out, any student with the matching word crosses it off their card.

- Select key words from a powerful speech like Martin Luther King's 'I Have A Dream'. Listen to a recording on CD or online audio file (try **www.americanrhetoric.com**). Students cross them off as they hear them. Use to identify key patterns of imagery.

- Alternatively, get them crossing off examples of persuasive techniques as they hear them in a speech, or examples of specific types of figurative language as in Teachit's *Key Stage 3/4>Skills>Lesson starters>Literary terms bingo*.

- Word class recognition: students have bingo cards with parts of speech on them instead of numbers. Caller calls out words which student writes into the appropriate box. When they think

they've got a full house, they leap in the air. Check out Teachit's *Key Stage 3>Skills>Sentence level work>Bingo!*

### What's the point?

It encourages attention to detail, concentration and rapid processing of information. And yeah, it's also a bit of fun to get attention at the start of a lesson, liven up a revision lesson or change the pace in a long scheme of work.

### Tricks of the trade

Maximise learning by interrogating the student's card for accuracy, testing their understanding, and getting the whole class involved in this discussion. Link it to follow up work that goes deeper and makes good use of the attention to detail you have just fostered – otherwise it really should just be kept for end of term fluff.

### Variations on a theme

- Put short questions in the boxes and everyone has got a slightly different reading comprehension task for any text you like. Then they can work together in groups to piece together the full set of answers and ideas.

- Use it as an ice breaker with a new class where students don't already know each other. Put attributes, hobbies, favourite things in the boxes, then students can play human bingo, moving round the class, introducing themselves and crossing off the squares by writing over the name of the student with that quality.

- Take digital photos of things you want students to look at on a trip or visit, and make visual bingo cards, with or without a linked set of questions.

### Whizzing it

Flash the items up on the IWB instead of pulling them out of a bag for big screen attention getting.

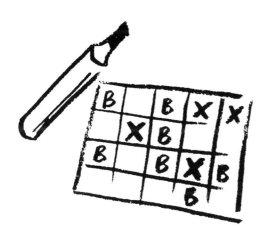

# Blockbusters

'I'd like a P please, Bob.'

## The basic idea

Just like that old telly programme, complete with the almost immortal line (well, for anyone over the age of 30) 'I'd like a P please, Bob'. There are 20 connected hexagrams on the board, in a five by four pattern. Each one has a letter on it. Students are in teams. They choose a hexagram/letter and have to answer a question correctly to win it. The question is in the format 'What W is the most north-westerly state in the USA?' The answer is always a word. If answered correctly, students win that hexagram. To win, they have to make a line from side to side (five hexagrams) or top to bottom (four hexagrams). Tactical blocking is good. See **www.ukgameshows.com** if you're feeling nostalgic and/or have no idea what I'm talking about…

## Applying it

- Good for revising key terms or new vocabulary providing you have enough items.

- Try revising important details of a set text; as long as there are one word answers Blockbusters will work. Check out Teachit's **Key Stage 3/4>Prose>Animal Farm by George Orwell>Animal Farm Blockbuster**.

- End of term wind-down with the fun-size Mars bar incentive to excellence.

### What's the point?

Gives feedback about which items need further revision. Puts students on the spot about how much they have learned, but in a fun way. A bit of competitive edge can encourage productive memory-dredging rather than the usual 'I dunno' of a wet Friday afternoon. Figuring out how to win develops on-the-feet and tactical thinking.

### Tricks of the trade

Can be played as a whole class but you need to organise it so that everyone gets a go. This is best done with competing pairs; as soon as one pair loses another steps up. You need to prevent observers shouting out the answers, so either gag them or give

them something to do. Inviting them to answer any question the contestants don't get right in exchange for a mini Mars bar usually does the trick. If that's likely to get too riotous, break it down into simultaneous quarter finals, with a questioner and a series of contestants. Then play the semi-final and final in the whole class context. Questioners can pair up for the semis as compensation for their duties, or you can give this role to students who will do anything not to compete.

### Variations on a theme

- When the students chorus 'what a rubbish game', or just because it might be an interesting thing to do anyway, challenge them to design a word game that is better.

- Teacher versus students adds an extra dimension, but for this you need to have got the students writing the questions first. Even better revision for them and no preparation for you…

### Whizzing it

Get the hexagon template projected up on the IWB. Have someone who gets out early using the colour fill function to keep track of the score. It's not hard to do (especially if you inveigle a student into creating it for you…) but it looks good.

# Brainstorming

Or whatever PC name it's got now

## The basic idea

Pick a topic and a focusing concept or key word. Set a relatively short time limit. Students tip the contents of their heads out in response to that concept or key word. The idea is not to edit anything at all out at this stage, only to capture it – usually on the board or a flipchart. Anything goes, and no judgement of it should be allowed. When, and only when, all thoughts have been exhausted, encourage reflection on what has been said or written. At this stage ideas can be joined up, scrubbed out, developed, in working towards a coherent set of ideas about the topic in question.

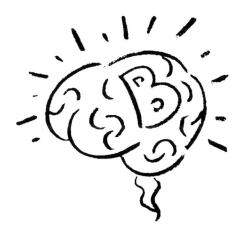

## Applying it

• So many zillions of uses it's hardly worth specifying any, but for developing lines of enquiry for essays beyond the obvious, for pooling phrases and ideas for creative writing on a particular theme, for sharing immediate personal responses to a poem, for capturing gut reactions to a controversial news item…

## What's the point?

It can help to access fresh ideas by going directly for immediate and unmediated thinking. Learning to suspend critical judgement for a while supports the development of creativity in a big way. It encourages students to seek a rich pool of ideas when working on any topic, rather than just settling for the first five ideas that come to mind. Once the ideas have been pooled, the process of selection and rejection encourages good critical debate.

## Tricks of the trade

This technique is vastly overused and often not done very effectively because too much judgement is allowed too early on. Like that, it becomes an exercise in guessing what's in the teacher's head, rather than liberating the student's own thinking. Resist very strongly the temptation to give any feedback such as 'good' or 'I like that' or 'what?!' Don't question or comment at all. Just capture what students say. This makes it a much tougher activity to do as a teacher, but the quality of thinking generated will make it worth the supreme effort of saying nothing! Let them do the selection and rejection and questioning and debate afterwards, and you can guide and steer as appropriate then!

### Variations on a theme

• Try getting students to do it individually in silence for a change, especially if you are looking to encourage a personal response, as to a poem.

• Another nice silent variation is to get students doing it in small groups on flipchart paper. Instead of all calling out their responses, they have a marker pen each and have to scribble their ideas down. Then they can discuss them, draw lines to connect things, annotate further, delete, etc.

• For group work, appoint an observer whose task is to feed back afterwards about the quality of the ideas and discussion process. A student with high levels of emotional intelligence, not necessarily your biggest boff. It's a nice opportunity to value other types of excellence.

### Whizzing it

This is what IWBs were made for, isn't it?…

# Card sorts

The simple pleasure of a pair of scissors

## The basic idea

Information about a text or topic is placed on a series of cards. Each group of students gets a set of cards. They have to sort them in some way to process the information and develop ideas.

## Applying it

- Cards with key quotations from a text on. Students to sort out which ones they would use to illustrate a particular theme.

- Cards with key words on which can be used to create statements about the text, as in Teachit's **Key Stage 4>Prose>Of Mice and Men by John Steinbeck>A table for recording impressions of the characters**.

- Cards with words on, to be sorted into word classes – just nouns and verbs, or the whole kit and caboodle. Make sure you include some that cross the boundaries (let's face it, it won't be hard, given the wondrous flexibility of the English language).

- Cards each illustrating one of Chaucer's *General Prologue* pilgrims. Students sort them into sequence, and then move them around to explore other patterns and connections between the characters.

- Try it as a stimulus for creative writing. Create sets of cards with images of people, places, objects, animals, weather, etc. Groups sort out which ones could go together to make a good story, generating as many different ideas as they can. Then individual or collective writing or storytelling.

## What's the point?

Putting information on cards makes it less fixed and certain than on a sheet of paper, allowing more scope for intellectual playfulness. The physical act of moving things around encourages experimentation and also makes kinaesthetically oriented students happy. Making the cards can also be a really calming therapeutic activity when all around you chaos rages.

## Tricks of the trade

The nicer the cards the more the students want to play with them. Bribing someone in your school/college to laminate them is well worth the effort as you'll then have a semi-indestructible re-usable resource. Semi-indestructible but very nickable so either make extra sets as Christmas gifts for all your colleagues, or lock them in a bank vault between lessons. Other than that, the only real trick to this simple activity is to make sure the task is a meaningful one. On the whole, that means setting a task where there are many possible ways of completing it, as that will stimulate the most productive discussion.

## Variations on a theme

- In the leisurely variation, you might get the students to make the cards themselves. For speed, have pre-prepared cards. But don't spend hours cutting them all up yourself (unless you need an excuse not to do several hours of marking). Give out the scissors and the sheets and get students to cut them up first.

- Different groups of students might work with different sets of cards. This could be to cover a range of focal points, e.g. groups working on cards related to different themes. Or it could be to give different students different levels of challenge.

## Whizzing it

For a simple card sort with a reasonably limited number of items, whack it on your IWB and get the students playing around with it on the board. Just use text boxes in Word to create the cards, then you can move them around. Or use Teachit's Flash card sorts (see **Whizzy things>Teachit Interactive** library).

# Carousel

Discussion that goes round in circles

## The basic idea

Students get divided in two. As a class, not individually as in some kind of magic show stunt (though that would certainly get their attention)… Half the class form an outer circle, half the class form an inner circle, facing each other. They're given a discussion question and a time limit. Inner ring student A1 talks about this to outer ring student B1. When the time is up, one of the rings is instructed to rotate x number of places to the left or right. So now inner ring student A7 is talking to outer ring student B1. They talk. Time's up. As many rotations as are useful.

### Applying it

- Use it to generate ideas about which bits of any suitable text were the scariest ahead of exploration of horror, the gothic, or how narrative tension is created. Works best if students have given some thought to the scariest bits in advance.

- Explore different points of view on a controversial topic before reading related non-fiction texts and writing persuasive pieces or preparing for a debate.

### What's the point?

Sometimes getting up and moving around unfreezes the brain, especially for kinaesthetically oriented students. The movement around the circles gets students talking to others in the class on a reasonably random basis, which can spark new perspectives and ideas. It engages every student in discussion, and it quickly draws out whatever range of ideas there is in the class.

### Tricks of the trade

Get the students to nail their coats to the classroom door as soundproofing for the rest of the department. But hey, if you don't do it for very long, they'll get over it and/or keep turning the telly up next door until you submit first! The idea is to keep it quick and lively so this really shouldn't be an issue. Don't whatever you do keep rotating until everyone has spoken to everyone else or you'll have some severe cases of rigor mortis to deal with.

### Variations on a theme

- Give different individual students different roles to play during the discussion, eg devil's advocate; give each ring a different role; or encourage different types of thinking with each rotation.

# Circuit training

A workout to tone up a variety of intellectual muscles

## The basic idea

Like doing circuits in the gym. Set up a series of stations around the room, each with a different kind of activity related to the text or topic. Students warm up, work round the stations in sequence, completing the tasks as best they can in the time available, then cool down to avoid overstretching any brain muscle before the next lesson. Depending on how you set it up, there could be one student working individually at a station, or four students working individually at a station; or they could be completing tasks collaboratively in pairs, triads or quads. Whatever.

## Applying it

- Each station has a different activity to explore a different poem from an anthology; at the end patterns and similarities are drawn together.

- Each station is a different kind of creative writing stimulus; at the end students choose the most successful one to develop further.

- Have different kinds of learning experience at each station. Check out Teachit's *Key Stage 3>Genre> Gothic Genre>Lesson ideas based on Gardner's Multiple Intelligences.* Same idea, same resource title in *Key Stage 3>Poetry>An introduction to poetry*. Got the gist? Very adaptable.

## What's the point?

To encourage the development of independent working in a structured and supported way. It also gives students a chance to tackle different types of tasks, some of which will be in the comfort zone of their preferred learning style or intelligence type, others of which will require them to develop greater flexibility. You can also get a lot of things done.

## Tricks of the trade

You need to make sure the activities are more or less self-explanatory. It's a good idea to have a prompt sheet at each station, but keep this short and snappy or it becomes like having to read all the rules on the new game you got for Christmas when you just want to play it. As with circuits in the gym, there needs to be a good level of variety in the tasks or energy and motivation levels start flagging. Think too about how you sequence them so there are changes of pace and intensity.

Then there's the timing. If you go laissez faire you'll end up with a queue at the exercise bike and no-one doing the bench presses. Give a time for each activity. In a small perfectly behaved class you can make these different times and get students to plan and organise themselves, perhaps with the support of a grid on the wall to monitor who's doing what when. In all other normal classes, it's a lot easier to set a fixed time limit before everyone rotates. That sometimes leads to students weeping that they didn't have time to finish something they were really enjoying, so allow time for them to choose one thing to develop further after the main section of the carousel. Or for homework.

## Variations on a theme

- If you set up more activities than you really need logistically, you can allow more scope for students to select activities. You can also differentiate more effectively. If, for example, you ask all students to do at least six out of nine activities that allows for superficial skaters to do more, and your deep and meaningfuls to go into more depth with a few.

- Alternatively, you might want to set the superficial skaters the challenge of ONLY doing six and your deep and meaningfuls the challenge of going faster. All depends what is best for their learning at any particular point.

- In the quick version, you choose simple five minute activities and rapid rotation; in the slower version, the activities are longer and more demanding and may be spread over a number of lessons.

## Whizzing it

Use laptops to make some of the stations a multimedia experience.

# Cloze

Popularity stranger than fiction

## The basic idea

A big bottle of real or virtual tippex. Remove some of the text. Students fill it back in, freehand, or from a list of alternative possibilities or from a list of fixed answers.

### Applying it

- Teachit's **Key Stage 3/4>Drama> Introduction to Shakespeare: background and biography> Shakespeare – a potted biography** has students completing the task using a fixed word list. If you like that kind of thing…

- For a freer hand and much more interesting discussion, get students inserting their own words and then comparing with the writer's choices, as in Teachit's **Key Stage 3> skills> Reading skills>The Da Vinci Code – the opening**.

- Explore the writer's drafting process. In Teachit's **Key Stage 4>Poetry> War poetry> Reconstructing a poem by Wilfred Owen** students choose between the words/phrases Wilfred Owen used in the four known drafts of *Anthem For Doomed Youth*.

- Explore grammatical issues with a wide open selection of words from which students choose to complete a passage. Excellent for underlining the fine balance of sentence structure and the occasional importance of small words.

- Also works for controlled practice of accurate use of features of spelling, punctuation and grammar.

### What's the point?

In its simplest form, filling in words from a fixed list, it engages students in reading with some level of engagement with the text. That's not to be knocked in some circumstances, and even AS/A2 students have been known to beg for more activities like this rather than having their heads fried with intellectual debate. It is, however, more interesting in its other mutations, when close critical reading comes into play, and/or creative experimentation with a writer's choices. For helping students see real drafting choices in action, both process and consequences, it can be excellent.

### Tricks of the trade

If you're creating a 'cloze' exercise with a fixed word list, road test it first to make sure it works. Any old geezer in the pub will do, or a student in another class. You need to make sure there aren't multiple semantic or grammatical possibilities that will only end up confusing students when you say 'er, no, although that works grammatically, actually it's wrong'. Other than that, make sure the level of challenge is appropriate to individual students otherwise it can either be deeply tedious for strong students or they finish it in three and a half seconds and have nothing to do but play with their piercings while waiting for everyone else to finish.

### Variations on a theme

- Get your hands on one of the comic book versions of *Macbeth*, or other Shakespeare play. Tippex the words out of the speech bubbles of a scene or section you want to focus on. As a pre-reading task, get students to add their own dialogue. And/or during the reading, get students to select key bits of dialogue from the text to go with each frame.

- Take a photo story and tippex the words out of that. Students can write their own dialogue as a creative activity in dialogue development. If they really get into it, give them a digital camera and let them produce one.

- Don't hog all the fun: get students creating their own cloze exercises and swapping them with their classmates.

### Whizzing it

Use the cloze activities available in the **Whizzy things>Teachit Interactive** library.

# Creative retelling

The infernal Lady Macbeth's diary

## The basic idea

Take a situation from a text. Retell the story in a different format or from another point of view, giving free rein to imaginative development. See also News Desk and Letters for creative retelling in these big hitting formats.

### Applying it

- Obituaries of characters. Try Spit Nolan in Teachit's **Key Stage 3>Prose>Spit Nolan by Bill Naughton>Writing Spit Nolan's obituary**.

- Every English teacher's favourite (apparently…), the character's diary. Way too many to list individually. Just type 'diary' into Teachit's search box and check em out. All the usual suspects are there - Romeo, Mr and Mrs Macbeth – but you'll find a few others too – Naledi from *Journey to Jo'burg*, Mina from *Skellig*, Lovell from *The Mistletoe Bough*.

- Police reports as in Teachit's resource on the events in an Agatha Christie story in **Key Stage 4>Prose>Wide reading: Detective stories>Police report based on 'Philomel Cottage'**. Combine if you like with the murderer's confession as in Teachit's **Key Stage 3/4>Poetry> Porphyria's Lover by Robert Browning>A short language/ literature unit of work**. Also witness statements as in Teachit's **Key Stage 3/4> Prose> Nightmare in Yellow by Fredric Brown>A guest's police statement.**

- Keep the genre, change the narrative point of view. Teachit's **Key Stage 3>Prose>Oliver Twist (NLS Y8) by Charles Dickens>First person narrative** has students rewriting events from Oliver's point of view.

- It's not just a lower school thing. Get Bathsheba Everdene and Sergeant Troy from *Far from the Madding Crowd* each describing their version of events in 'The Hollow Amid the Ferns' and you'll be linking nicely to work on Freudian perspectives for A2.

### What's the point?

It encourages close reading both for explicit textual detail and between the lines. It provides students who enjoy imaginative writing an alternative to essays. It also helps students to 'feel'

the significance of narrative point of view and the effect it has on our understanding of the story. If anyone tells you it's an inferior option, point out that Tom Stoppard didn't do too badly with it in his writing of *Rosencrantz and Guildenstern Are Dead*.

### Tricks of the trade

Make sure students understand the conventions of the genre they are doing the creative retelling in and the creative purpose of the activity. If this isn't clear, some of them will just paraphrase the events of the text working on the mistaken basis that it's a reading comprehension activity. Pick good passages where there is a lot of scope for imaginative development, or which will produce a good contrast with the original.

### Variations on a theme

- For extension, some advanced students might be interested to explore published creative transformations such as Stoppard's and challenged to produce a drama in this way. It's the spin-off mini-series concept they are all familiar with…

- Try it for speaking and listening too: I saw an inspired Jerry Springer show format with characters from the *Lion, the Witch and the Wardrobe*. Similarly, Teachit's **Key Stage 4>Drama>An Inspector Calls by JB Priestley> Speaking & Listening: Chat show - who is to blame?** Great fun with excellent opportunities for audience participation.

- Save the work a previous class did on this. Then if you're short of time, or your students all hate creative writing, they can still explore the effects of alternative points of view. Produces lively discussion about the quality of other students' work too!

- For extra extension, challenge them to change a larger section of a text with omniscient third person narration to multiple narration; or to make a reliable narrator unreliable.

# Cut Ups

Sequencing activities (and more scissor action...)

## The basic idea

Take a text of any kind: a poem, a story, a speech, a set of instructions, a summary of a story. Chop it up into little pieces – lines, stanzas, paragraphs, etc – and mix them up. Students then have to put them in the correct sequence.

### Applying it

- Sequence the lines of a poem or lines of a speech to get students working on the text from the inside out. Check out Teachit's **Key Stage 4>Poetry> Poems from different cultures> 'What were they like?' Introduction activities**. Also works well with Andrew Marvell's 'To His Coy Mistress' or Donne's 'The Flea' to explore the distinctive structure of logical argument.

- Sequence events from a text to get students' hands on the plot structure. Try Teachit's **Key Stage 3/4>Drama> Richard III>The plot** and **Key Stage 5>Drama>Othello>Sequence the plot**.

- To develop critical thinking at higher levels, give students the pieces of a logical argument to sequence, as in Teachit's **Key Stage 5>Skills>Essay writing>Excellent essay writing**.

### What's the point?

Sequencing tasks encourage a close attention to detail, and a focus on the way that texts are linked together with threads of meaning, and language and form. This can generate really good discussion of textual cohesion and coherence, though you might not want to call it that…

### Tricks of the trade

Choose a text with sufficient challenge to make it interesting: you can always have a system of clues to provide additional support if some students need it. Literal chopping up with a pair of scissors is fine, but invest a pleasant half hour in creating laminated cards and you've got a recyclable resource that will save you time in the long run. Or invest a pleasant smile in a resources technician who may do it for you…

Then it's really about what you do with this. It's far more creative and interesting to discuss the 'incorrect' answers than it is merely to stamp gold stars on the foreheads of those who got it right. If you probe the 'incorrect' answers you will frequently find (unless you have a class full of stroppy refuseniks) precious nuggets of ambiguity and possibility that generate insightful responses way beyond the simple sequencing task you started with.

### Variations on a theme

- Chop a poem up into lines and phrases as you like. Give the pieces to the students with the task of creating a poem they find pleasing. The task is NOT to attempt to guess what the 'real' poem was, but to play around with its language. Set whatever 'rules' you like: they must use every word; they can substitute any or a fixed number of words; they can omit as many or a fixed limit of words. Explore the poems created and only when that's done, compare with the original.

- For work on the plot, try combining it with **Flowcharts** to get them producing diagrams of the sequence they have identified. Or comic strips.

### Whizzing it

Use Teachit's many Flash sequencing activities in the **Whizzy things> Interactive library** And/or put each of the chopped up sections into a text box in Word and you have a ready-made activity for use on the interactive whiteboard. Useful for working through the answers collectively.

# Debate

## Let rip the tub-thumping passion

## The basic idea

Always looks easier than it actually is to get a really good one going. As with most things in teaching that look easy, it's largely down to the preparation. But the basic idea is simple: students take opposing positions on a topic and seek to persuade their opponents and/or an audience, of the truth, logic, and moral virtue of their line of argument. And/or they seek to destroy the truth, logic and moral virtue of their opponent's line of argument. The outcome can be decided by voting, or by judges, or by a mixture of the two. It can be a fairly informal affair, or a rule governed system. For information on the latter see comprehensive descriptions at **http://en.wikipedia.org/wiki/Debate**

### Applying it

• Debate home schooling from a set of given positions in Teachit's ***Key Stage 3>Prose>Skellig by David Almond> Mina's education: the home schooling debate***

• Teachit's ***Key Stage 4>Media & Non-Fiction>Let Him Have It!>The Death Penalty – writing to persuade*** has students writing speeches for and against the restoration of the death penalty. Do the debate as well as/instead.

• For a fantastic selection of topics and motions that could build into all sorts of interesting projects involving persuasive speech and writing, see **www.idebate.org>Database**

### What's the point?

It encourages logical argument in which reasoning and evidence are brought to the fore. Rhetorical language may be employed to enhance the effect, but students quickly learn that style without substance does not often win the argument.

### Tricks of the trade

What you don't want to end up with is everyone shouting all at once, and in the heat of the moment that can easily happen. Although it takes more preparation, holding a very formal debate puts controls on who can speak when, and if you put a student in charge of keeping order rather than you, additional important lessons can be learned about how authority is effectively exercised. Another option is to have a symbolic Mace type thing and to insist that only the person holding it can speak. When the discussion is over, always debrief the class, exploring for each person how they felt, and have a follow up activity to draw together what has been learned.

### Variations on a theme

• Give some students the challenge of debating from a point of view they do not personally hold. This can help to encourage intellectual flexibility in those who tend to think their opinion is always right, and is a different challenge for gifted blaggers.

• For a short and sweet variation, give students starting points such as a list of key arguments for development and not much preparation time. In the full monty, first allow plenty of time for research, have formal speech writing and time to rehearse these, and build in an opportunity to identify counter-arguments and rebuttals.

• To decide who is on which side, ask students to line up in order of the strength of their opinion, from strongly agree to strongly disagree. The third on the left take one side of the debate, the third on the right take the other, the third in the middle get to judge. To prevent mayhem, have a quiet moment in which they visualise where on the line they want to stand, then get them to move there one by one.

• Hold a boxing debate. Two opponents go into the ring, metaphorically speaking. They have a timed bout of debate which the audience scores, either using their observational judgement or a pre-determined set of criteria. At the end of the round, their trainers can give them advice and suggestions for the next round. Off they go again. Either the referee declares a knock-out at some point, or it gets decided on scores. Play it how you like!

### Whizzing it

Oh go on then, you know you want to project an image of a boxing ring on the big screen, just because you can…

# Decision trees

Kind of diagram showing options/decisions

## The basic idea

Read up to the point at which a character in a text faces a major dilemma. Use a tree diagram to identify the decisions they could make at this juncture and to explore the consequences of these. The easiest way to explain this is to show an example. In the one on page 26, some of the options facing Cathy in chapter 9 of *Wuthering Heights*, and their possible outcomes, are shown in diagrammatic form. The squares represent decisions faced; the circles represent possible consequences. Once the diagram has been drawn, explore the options: which one would you take? which one do you think the character will take? Then read on to find out what decision the character does take and how it ends up.

### Applying it

• Macbeth's moral dilemma after his visit to the witches.

• The options facing Stanley at the end of chapter 30 of Louis Sachar's *Holes*, after Zero has run away from the camp. Or how about options facing Christopher in Mark Seddon's *Curious Incident of the Dog in the Nighttime* when he finds out his mother is still alive?

• The decisions facing Frankenstein the moment his creation comes to life, and the possible outcomes of those. Or the decisions facing George in Steinbeck's *Of Mice And Men* once he finds Curley's wife is dead.

### What's the point?

It gets students thinking imaginatively about the way the plot could go at a particular point. On a simple level this can help to generate an excited anticipation about the reading to come, and to develop the idea that fiction is the product of choices the writer has made. On a more complex level, it can help students to empathise with the moral dilemmas faced by a character, and to explore the significance of the plotting decisions made by the writer.

*(continued over)*

### Tricks of the trade

Show an example to illustrate what you want the students to produce, or work as whole class to create the diagram together.

### Variations on a theme

• This technique can also be used to map out possible plot lines for students' own imaginative writing. Get them to select or create a character. Give the character a moral dilemma (students' choice, your choice, or random choice from a set of dilemmas cards as with a game like Scruples). Draw a diagram to show the consequences of all the possible actions that could be taken and decisions made. Encourage students to explore comedy, tragedy, horror, etc. When they have all been explored, develop the most interesting, funny, outrageous, scariest, most moving, or whatever, into a story.

• Combine this activity with research into the social and historical context in which the text is set, to ensure that the options and consequences are an accurate reflection of the times. Otherwise you get Cathy choosing to don leather trousers and a couple of firearms and shooting everyone down in an action fantasy sequence.

(Though that would, of course, be really cool…)

• For students who need more support, give them a diagram with some parts filled in and the rest of the labels to write on, as a kind of fancy cloze exercise.

### Whizzing it

For once, this is something that is easier to produce using the interactive whiteboard software than it is on a PC. Drawing the lines and shapes is easy in Word, but annotating them isn't, so revel in the big screen multimedia experience. Go bigger by doing it with hyperlinks instead of lines.

## Options facing Cathy in chapter 9 of *Wuthering Heights*

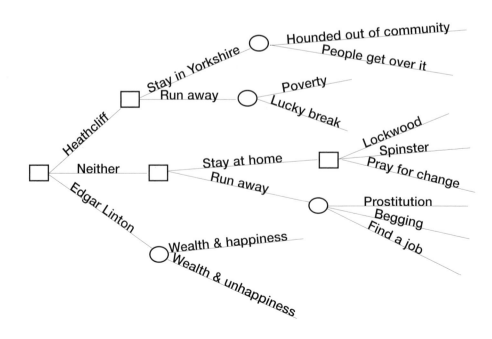

# Degrees of belief

Different types of scales for weighing opinions

## The basic idea

Use a continuum to determine the extent to which students hold certain opinions or beliefs. Mark positions on a line, have a classroom swingometer, get them lining up according to the strength of their convictions. Use it with a single continuum as the basis for starting or judging a debate. Use it with multiple scales to judge different aspects of a situation, a text or a character. Use lines from smiley faces to sad faces; statements such as 'strongly agree' to 'strongly disagree'; numbers from one to five, or one to ten; lines between opposing ideas.

### Applying it

• Get students to show where they think different characters lie along lines between opposing characteristics, eg cautious to hasty, wise to foolish, most moral to least moral. Explore if and how these positions change during the course of the narrative. For a nice variation try the character personality wheel in Teachit's *Key Stage 3> Skills>Reading skills>What is character?*

• Take a list of literary themes and get students judging degrees of importance to the text, ahead of detailed focus on those they think are the most significant.

• Get students to physically identify where they stand in a debate on a controversial topic by lining up according to the strength of their affinity to one side or the other.

### What's the point?

It generates good discussion as students work out where on the line to put their mark. It gets them committing to a belief or opinion, and from there you have a foundation for developing an argument or an interpretation. It represents very tangibly the important idea that most debates are not black and white but many shades of grey between.

### Tricks of the trade

Don't make it too easy. The longer the line, the more shades of grey there are. Don't define these shades of grey, let them do that and justify their position as this is a far richer kind of learning.

### Variations on a theme

• Go multi-dimensional. Well, okay, two dimensional is probably enough. This produces a cross with one set of qualities or beliefs going from top to bottom, and one set going from left to right. If you do this with pairs of character qualities that students think are of most significance to the story, they can then plot where each character lies on this graph.

• Go circular. Draw a bullseye on the floor. Get students to stand on it according to the strength of their agreement with a proposition about a text or topic. The more they agree, the closer they stand to the bullseye. Can get very cosy.

• Some students will be ready to mark their opinions on predetermined scales; some will be ready to produce their own scales. This can produce interesting perspectives, especially if charged with the task of going beyond what you have produced.

• For imaginative writing development, use this technique to develop ideas for a story about a person who one day completely changed their mind about something. Plot the events of this day along the line.

### Whizzing it

Continuum lines and bullseyes can all be whacked up on the interactive whiteboard very easily for annotation. Create some little character icons and get students moving them about along the lines to show what they think. Or dots that they each place to show their opinion, then count the dots for a class survey of opinions. Hours of touchy feely fun (unless you have the other kind of board, in which case, first find your pen gizmo thing…)

# Director's cuts

## Cutting scenes and doubling up actors

## The basic idea

Take a play. Impose restrictions about its performance: fewer actors than the number of parts, and/or a strict time limit, and/or a specific audience such as children. Students have to be the director, deciding what roles to double up or cut, and which scenes to axe in part or completely. Then they get to justify their choices and the consequences of these, compare them with each other's decision, and with actual directors' decisions.

### Applying it

• Consider how a small theatre company might produce a play with a fairly large cast, such as Timberlake Wertenbaker's *Our Country's Good*. Lots of information available about how it was originally cast with double-up roles.

• Use to soup up existing Director's Notes activities for Key Stage 3 and 4 work on set scenes/plays.

• Set AS/A2 students to work gleefully on the whoppers like *King Lear* or *Hamlet* that have been plaguing them for weeks/months/years.

### What's the point?

It encourages students to think about the essential components of the play. An excellent activity when they're all moaning that it's too long, as it's actually quite difficult to cut anything without heartache and angst. Or major loss of meaning. It also encourages students to think as directors and to see the text as a working script, to be played around with in order to produce a performance, rather than a sacred work of art to be preserved in aspic. That's healthy…

### Tricks of the trade

Set clear parameters for the cuts: a specific performance time or length, or a specific number of actors. This gives a definite goal to the task that can help to keep it sharply focused. If you really want to make the point about the non-sanctity of drama texts, get them cutting it up literally and pasting the bits they're keeping together into a new version. Maybe an e-text version you can print off and photocopy for this purpose would be better than the brand new set of books your head of department just bought you…

### Variations on a theme

• Do it in reverse. Give them a cut script and get them to find what has been left out. Then explore the consequences of these decisions. Check out Teachit's **Key Stage 3/5>Drama>Henry V>15 minute Henry V**.

• Focus instead or as well on decisions actually made by directors, comparing a full length, every word version with a medium sized one and a short one. Shakespeare is always a fruitful source for this. Try Branagh's 242 minute Hamlet in contrast with the 26 minute *Shakespeare: The Animated Tales* version.

### Whizzing it

Get them cutting and pasting without the mess. And/or producing a colour-coded edition of an e-text version to show which bits have been excluded in different productions on stage or screen. With annotations in drop down comment boxes to explore the effects of these cuts.

# DIY study guides
Put the rest out of business

## The basic idea

Instead of students spending money on sets of notes that are never quite what they need and only serve to support the deeply held conviction that the answer is out there instead of in here, get them collaborating as a class to write their own. Adapt the format from a handful of style models, divvy up the work appropriately amongst the class members and away you go. Cut and paste all the pages together into one document with a cool cover (even better, get a student to do it…), whack it into reprographics, and everyone will have their very own home grown study guide.

### Applying it

• This works well with any text but it works best with classes which have a moderate level of anxiety about it. If they're finding the text straightforward why bother producing a study guide? If they're really out of their depth, this kind of hurling into the deep end may result in drowning.

### What's the point?

It gets students taking direct action to improve their own learning, and encourages them to see that this is far more powerful than passive consumerism. They have to work collaboratively to get the job done and at a high standard to make it worthwhile. Usually, the fact that they are going to use the finished product for real study purposes makes that happen naturally.

### Tricks of the trade

This is all about managing the task so that it doesn't became a sprawling great beast of a project. Agree format and page lengths before you start. Make sure different students get an appropriate level of challenge, either through setting easier/more difficult tasks, or longer/shorter tasks, or by throwing in added dimensions. Then set a non-negotiable deadline for completion: if it's not finished, they will let the class down. Keep close tabs on progress and chivvy hard as the deadline approaches. If you have time, get groups of students reviewing each other's sections and then redrafting their own in the light of constructive criticism, additions and amendments.

### Variations on a theme

• Experiment with other popular formats, such as 'A Beginner's Guide to….'

• It's far easier to do if the text you are studying doesn't already have a study guide available in book or online form, as students really do have to think for themselves and create something from scratch. Don't get stressed if one does exist – use the opportunity at the start for students to test it to destruction against possible essay titles, find its limitations and come up with a better design.

### Whizzing it

A very simple idea: instead of giving students the finished product in paper form, email it to them. Then they can save it and customise it in their own way for revision, adding bits, deleting them, rewriting, illustrating or whatever. Far more active process of revision than simply reading a booklet.

# Eagle eye
Spot the deliberate mistakes

## The basic idea

Take a text the students should be familiar with in some way and corrupt it. Students have to spot the deliberate mistakes

## Applying it

• The timeless task of spotting spelling, punctuation and grammatical infelicities in a text uses this technique. Just liven it up by making the text one that students actually want to read instead of the letter to ageing dowager Aunt Flora that we all had to correct at school. Try Teachit's **Key Stage 3>Prose>Boy (NLS Y7) by Roald Dahl>Letter from Boy to Mother** or **Key Stage 3>Prose>Madame Doubtfire>Missing Punctuation**.

• Useful for essay development work. Start with a paragraph from a good answer and corrupt the sequence, or chop out the quotation. Build up to a sequence of paragraphs from which you have chopped out all the links, or squidge them together to corrupt the paragraphing itself. Try Teachit's **Key Stage 3>Skills>Sentence level work – grammar and punctuation> Correction exercise – The Iron Man**.

## What's the point?

It encourages close attention to detail in the hope that correcting someone else's work will help students internalise the issues and not replicate them in their own writing. The question of how much this kind of consciousness-raising translates into practice is debatable, but always worth a try, as you do get lightbulb moments from it sometimes.

## Tricks of the trade

The level of challenge is the difference between this being a useful activity and not being so, therefore well worth going the extra mile on differentiation. Think about giving different students a version of the text which highlights their particular issue. This is not necessarily anything to do with intellectual ability: the dodgy spellers might be in one group with one text; those with a penchant for over-ornate curlicues of phrasing in another. It is important that each student identifies what they have learned from this: one memorable and important thing is enough.

## Variations on a theme

• For development of attention to descriptive detail, use spot the difference cartoons (just google it) as a starter. Instead of circling the differences, have students describe them. Choose good cartoons and you've got a starting point for stories. What happened before? What happened next? At last, a useful purpose for those spot the difference cartoons used in health and safety training courses…

## Whizzing it

Have the documents for correction on the network so that students can make changes on screen, or highlight and put suggested corrections and amendments in comment boxes. They could then print these off for comparison between groups before a final 'model answer' is produced. Alternatively or as well, whack it up on the IWB and get different groups annotating their corrections in different colours, then compare.

# Echoing

Experimenting with multiple voices

## The basic idea

Students work in groups to prepare a reading of a scene or speech or poem, in which two people take each part. One does the main reading, the other provides echoes of key words or phrases. Work it up into a performance. Compare. Discuss.

### Applying it

- Works well with all the classic war poems for really bringing out some of the shocking and emotive elements.

- Give Lady Macbeth some echoes in readings/performances of the sleepwalking scene.

- Try it with Martin Luther King's 'I Have a Dream' to draw out the patterns of language and the oratorical power.

- Go for a complete nervous breakdown of an echoing performance of key scenes of *A Streetcar Named Desire* .

### What's the point?

It engages students in a close reading of the text. In choosing which bits to echo, they naturally highlight the most interesting features of language which can later be analysed. It draws attention to the spokenness of these text types and encourages students to play around with this in creative ways. It is another way of sneaking in a bit of performance-type work for the dramatically challenged.

### Tricks of the trade

Choose good texts to work with where there is plenty of scope for original creative interpretation. It is well worth having a practice go in the whole class context, to make sure everyone has the right end of the stick before they start. Can involve lots of noise so think about where, when and what gift you are buying for your classroom neighbour.

### Variations on a theme

- Think non-musical Gladys Knight and the Pips. Instead of just one person echoing key words and phrases, experiment with different numbers and different patterns of repetition, echoing and choral speaking. Let their imaginations go to town. If they're any good, and they want to sing, well, why not?

- Have different groups working on different poems or scenes, or do the same and then compare interpretations and decisions made.

- Produce director's notes type version of the text, annotated to show what and why, and the interpretation of the text that their choices have constructed.

### Whizzing it

Produce audio recordings of the work created and podcast to the world. Or use to create multimedia animated versions of the texts.

# Endings
Rewrites and alternatives

## The basic idea

Take a text with a definite ending, happy or sad. Rewrite it the other way round. See what happens, to the structure of the text, to interpretations, to the real-world issue of reader enjoyment. Writing and discussion for a whole month of Sundays.

### Applying it

• If you're doing a controlled class reading of a text, stop when you get to the crisis point and get the students to write two endings, one happy, one sad. Get strong students to write an open ending. Use to stimulate discussion about their interpretations and what they prefer, what clues either way there might be in the text, and then read on in a high state of excitement for what comes next.

• Read the *Guardian* feature article on revised endings, 'Star-crossed lovers no more' (03.03.06). Go to **www.guardian.co.uk>*search*>** (type in) 'Star-crossed lovers no more' this title in inverted commas. If you're working on *Romeo and Juliet*, *Tess of the D'Urbervilles*, *Anna Karenina* (anyone?!) or *1984*, are these the right alternative endings? How would your students have them end?

• For *King Lear*, write the happy ending and compare with Nahum Tate's 1681 version, accessible at **http://andromeda.rutgers.edu/~jlyn ch/Texts/tatelear.html**.

• Surely *Pride and Prejudice* would be much improved by immediate divorce, financial ruin, alcoholic destruction, pregnancy, murderous violence, and a high body count? Sounds sacrilegious, I know, but it can draw out very powerfully all the things Jane Austen doesn't say in the novel but are there as a dark swirling undercurrent.

### What's the point?

Hours of family entertainment for a start, but in the process excellent discussion of how we value literature, and how we are each positioned in relation to dominant literary values. It encourages creativity, and the notion that the literary text is not some hallowed ground to

genuflect before in solemn piety but to be grappled with and made messy in order to make our own meanings and understandings.

### Tricks of the trade

The writing can be a lot of fun, especially done collaboratively at least in some stages. Performances and/or readings can provoke fantastic discussion as students engage in each other's non-conformity and experimentation. But you do need to do some work after the fun bit in drawing out what has been learned, both about the specific text and about literature and literary values. This isn't hard, but you need to plan for it and have good follow-up discussion questions.

### Variations on a theme

• The fast and easy version involves students just writing an outline of the ending; the more complex and time consuming version has students writing their version in the same style as the writer.

• Follow up the article in the *Guardian* mentioned above with a survey of reader preferences about happy and sad endings. Get students writing letters to local or school book clubs with the findings, giving a presentation to the local or school librarian, etc.

• To mix it up a bit, try using storyboards for students to work out their endings on. For focus, constrain the number of shots they can use. I find five a good number for most things, if only because that fits nicely on a single sheet of paper...

• Link to more complex work on comedy and tragedy, or on how the ending is a context for our re-reading of a text (or indeed, how any foreknowledge of the kind of ending is a context for our initial reading).

# Examples... examples...

Because you can never get enough

## The basic idea

Students start with a framework of ideas about an aspect of the subject which they then have to illustrate with examples. This is similar to a **Quote quest** (page 110) , but it's focused more on objective exemplification of relatively factual concepts, not finding quotations to justify subjective interpretations.

### Applying it

• Find examples of types of imagery as in Teachit's very adaptable **Key Stage 3>SATs>Macbeth Act 2>Finding imagery in Act 2 Scenes 1 and 2**.

• Equally adaptable for other texts and key stages, Teachit's **Key Stage 5>Prose>Cold Comfort Farm> Comedy in Cold Comfort Farm** has students finding passages from the novel to exemplify different types of humour used in the novel.

• In a similar vein, introduce students to ideas about characterisation technique, give them cards with a range of examples from different novels, get them matching examples to techniques.

• As a way into reading, have students finding textual evidence to support a set of factual notes about a text, as in Teachit's **Key Stage 5>Poetry>John Keats>To Charles Cowden Clarke**.

### What's the point?

It gives students a secure starting point, where such things can be said to exist in a subject like English. This can make a welcome change for some students from the usual shifting sands of subjectivity. Finding or correctly matching examples requires close attention to detail and careful discrimination. It emphasises the importance of illustrating ideas with examples in order to help clarify them, which can be a useful activity in building an awareness of the *point* of all that PEE talk.

### Tricks of the trade

It can take a long time to find good examples in a long text because it entails a lot of thumbing through the book, wondering where 'that bit' was. So, if you're short of time it's worth doing it as a matching exercise with prepared cards. Just make sure it's not too easy or there won't be any richness to the discussion. Include some ambiguous cards, some that cross over between categories or ideas, and make sure the answer isn't predictable (e.g. by making the same number of cards go with each idea, or colour coding them).

### Variations on a theme

• Once students have illustrated all the ideas, encourage creative thinking by getting them to critique the framework. Are there ideas that have been omitted? Any that are in unnecessarily? Redesign it as required. Throw in a few spanners with other ways of looking at the concept if your class can handle it.

• Get students pooling the examples they have all picked and then filtering them to find the best ones. Makes for lively discussion.

### Whizzing it

Matching examples to framework works well on the interactive whiteboard, with electronic 'cards' manipulated and amended at will, saved and printed off.

# Exchange and mart

Collective and co-operative exchange of ideas

## The basic idea

In groups or individually, students brainstorm a set of key ideas. They set out their wares on post-its on a flipchart market stall or similar. Then they go to market, eyeing up everybody else's wares and trading their ideas. Their task is to end up with a better set of ideas than they started with. They're not allowed to give ideas away: everything must be a trade though its terms are negotiable. Each person or group must trade at least one idea. Any individual idea can be traded many times. Judge the best set of ideas produced – even better, have a vote on them.

### Applying it

- Livens up essay planning and practice, with lots of discussion about the best ideas. Beats doing timed essays for revision.

- Liven up reading comprehension by giving out a wide range of questions and getting students to trade for the ones they want to answer. What will they go for? One big tough question or lots of little easy ones?

- When revising an anthology, give out copies of the texts and get students trading for a set they will produce a presentation on.

- Do it as a creative writing development activity. Individually, students brainstorm ideas from a single stimulus and then trade them to develop a really great starting point for writing.

### What's the point?

It gets students thinking about the information they most want, discriminating between ideas and making a commitment to them. It gets them sharing ideas and seeing what other people are thinking. All of that is far better than mournful cries of 'but I don't know what to write...' from the back of the room as most students can be persuaded to write something if they know they can swap it later. A different kind of talent will emerge in this kind of activity: call it hustling, call it negotiation skills, but let it flourish.

### Tricks of the trade

Let the entrepreneurial spirit roll and this can be a really good laugh as students wheel and deal. How far will they go to get the perfect idea? Will they try and amass lots of ideas or try to end up with as few as possible? Within the general parameters let constructive 'cheating' happen – the other name for that is creative thought and interesting things can end up happening when that's given space in a classroom. If it bombs, so what? Get the class evaluating why and learning from it.

### Variations on a theme

- To add an extra dimension of challenge, you take part too, trading some higher level or left-field ideas with those who want them. Doesn't matter what you end up with... Or play it so that your goal is to 'buy up' all the rubbish ideas so you can discreetly bin them.

# Eye witness

Visual memory and attention to descriptive detail

## The basic idea

An eye witness eye witnesses something: a photograph, a text, a video clip. A detective interviews him/her to find out as much as possible what it was like, then has to track down possible culprits and try to identify the correct one.

### Applying it

• As a pre-reading task, show a video/DVD clip of Macbeth stabbing Duncan to the eye-witness(es). Detectives have a snapshot of each member of the dramatis personae as possible suspects. They are not allowed to show their snapshots to the eye witness, but can ask as many questions as they need to eliminate different suspects from their enquiry.

• As a starting point for creative writing: in pairs, the eye witness sees an interesting or unexpected portrait (images from fine art or photography – in a gallery, a book or an online collection). Their detailed description helps the detective find the image in the gallery and creates a character profile. Then they collaborate to invent a crime story in which this character is either the suspect or the victim, or indeed the detective.

### What's the point?

It's about the development of visual memory and attention to detail, exploring alternatives in decision making, shared problem solving, and the practice of oral description and interviewing. Playing detectives is always fun for ardent problem solvers.

### Tricks of the trade

You need to think about what the eye witness(es) will be doing when they're not being interviewed. The trick is to make the challenge hard enough so that the detectives need to keep coming back to ask supplementary questions. Another trick is to get your eye witnesses throwing a few role-playing loops, with a bit of false memory syndrome here and a suddenly remembered fact there.

### Variations on a theme

• Let the detectives get their revenge on the eye witnesses at the end. Make sure the eye witnesses only have a glimpse of the suspect at the start. The detectives do their job as described, but also put together an identity parade of closely related possibilities, from which the eye witness has to correctly identify the original. With the Macbeth task, use snapshots of Macbeth stabbing Duncan from different productions.

• Do it with or without the extra scaffolding of clues according to the range of abilities in the class. Additional scaffolding can be provided by giving weaker detectives a choice between a fixed number of options rather than completely free rein.

• Having identified the murderer and the victim, get students to skim read to identify the correct scene in the text.

### Whizzing it

Identity parades can be done as animated PowerPoint presentations.

# Family trees
## Genealogy for beginners

## The basic idea

For our purposes (and not hard things involving mathematical probability) the idea of tree diagrams is to show the structural relationships between things. In English studies, we're really talking about family trees (and maybe a few grammar trees for language study if you're daring). Start at the top and work downwards until everything is accounted for.

### Applying it

• Family trees can be very useful in helping students keep track of who's who in a long novel, especially those with complicated family dynamics. Or just as a nice activity in getting students to write thumbnail character sketches. Check out this example for the Harry Potter novels: **http://en.wikipedia.org>***Search***>** ***Relatives of Harry Potter***.

• Try personal family tree diagrams as a way in to all sorts of auto/biographical writing. For language study, get them writing mini language profiles of each person as a way of exploring their individual language heritage. For creative writing, get them unearthing the most interesting character for straightforward historical narratives or 'Who Do You Think You Are?' style documentaries.

• Grammar trees bring a visual dimension to clause analysis for language study. Not everyone's cup of Darjeeling but deeply satisfying for the logically minded…

### What's the point?

It gets students sorting through large bodies of information and organising it in a concise and structured fashion that allows a comprehensive overview. It can help to develop logical thinking with precise analysis of connections, concise expression and hierarchical sequencing of ideas. Illustrated ones look nice too…

### Tricks of the trade

Show students what you mean first, especially if you're doing grammar trees or any of the souped up variations. Other than that it's a pretty straightforward activity that students generally enjoy, as long as they haven't done it thirty-eight times in the last term. Have extra challenges up your sleeve for the fast and furious, or link it to a written outcome they can get cracking on with.

### Variations on a theme

• It works just as well with soaps, and all kinds of family-based comedies and dramas. The 'who's who' family tree article is a popular telly guide sub-genre.

• Give students different kinds of character profiles to add to their family trees: try their goal in the novel, their hopes and fears, their secrets.

• For a tougher challenge, get students producing a 'family tree' that shows the structural connections between every character in the text.

### Whizzing it

Get students producing illustrated family trees for the school/college intranet. Their own or novel-related. To check out the competition, see what Wilbur Smith's webmaster has done at **www.wilbursmithbooks.com >***Family trees***.

# Feel the rhythm

Clapping, banging and running around - all in a good cause

## The basic idea

Getting students to appreciate the rhythm and metre of a piece of writing is not easy. It's okay when a poem belongs to the Humpty Dumpty school of rhythmic regularity, but anything more subtle and there is intellectual carnage in the classroom. Except that most students have at least a basic grasp of musical rhythm, and if you can tap into that understanding you stand a good chance of getting somewhere. So, clapping is good, banging on the table (for once) is good, rhythmic pacing of the classroom/gym/back field is good, percussion instruments are good…

### Applying it

- Before you even look at a text, get students experimenting with rhythms that convey different moods, get them identifying what patterns of beats and off-beats constitute different rhythms. Get them changing from one rhythm to another, sometimes stopping suddenly and holding their pose for a second before changing. Get them describing how that feels. And just when they've got the hang of it, blow their minds with how writers do all that with words.

- Start with poems with very marked rhythms. A few faves include: Hillaire Belloc's 'Tarantella'; G.K. Chesterton's 'The Rolling English Road'; W.H. Auden's 'Night Train'; and John Masefield's 'Sea Fever'.

- Move them on to more subtle uses of rhythm. The emotion of Auden's 'Funeral Song' ('Stop all the clocks…') keeps undermining the surface control and dignity of the persona. It's all there in the rhythm, and with the film tie-in to boot (*Four Weddings And A Funeral*) it's a timeless classic of a lesson in poetic form.

- Try comparing Macbeth's 'Stay you imperfect speakers' speech with 'She should have died hereafter'. Subtle disruptions and variations to the iambic pentameter help to signal the change.

### What's the point?

Connecting a difficult concept to knowledge students already have breaks down some of the barriers to learning about it in English. Those who can't 'see' it in the words on the page or 'hear' it in their reading can use their bodily intelligence to 'feel' poetic rhythm instead. Wordsworth wrote poetry when he was out walking in order to feel the rhythm of his thoughts so there is nothing dumbed-down or inappropriate about this approach.

### Tricks of the trade

This is not for making it up as you go along unless you have the classroom control of Darth Vader. Ordinary mortals need to structure it carefully to keep it focused on the points about rhythm that you are trying to teach. It can't just be aimless running around or noise making. You might do sequences of rhythm tasks with calm time in between to reflect on what is being learned, or you might give students specific rhythm problems to puzzle out and then present for discussion. Negotiating use of the gym, drama studio, music room or back field is worth the time, effort and bribes because you will waste far less breath hushing students up every three and a half seconds.

### Variations on a theme

- Link to creative writing to get the students experimenting with rhythm and metre in their own writing.

- Move straight to the top of the students' league table of teachers with some work on song lyrics. What relationships are there between musical rhythm and lyrical rhythm? Are the best song lyrics as rhythmically accomplished as the best poems, or are they lazy, leaving it to the music to do the work? Those are challenging questions whatever their popularity value…

- Invite students to find or create a piece of music to play as a suitable soundtrack to the poem or speech, and to explain their choice.

### Whizzing it

Whack the text up on the IWB and get students working collaboratively to colour code it with the rhythm and identify significant patterns and variations. Give pairs or small groups a line or section each, then moderate in the whole class forum.

# Film makers

## Hands on story-making

## The basic idea

Give the students a video camera of whatever sort you can lay your hands on. Beg, bribe or borrow from the Media department. Record stuff. Edit. Play. Discuss. Use it for simple playback, discussion and evaluation purposes. Add clips to written documents, or project in class for presentation and/or comparison with other students' work.

### Applying it

• Get students making their own narratives up from a brief, as in Teachit's *Key Stage 4>Media & Non-Fiction>Short Films>Making short films – student activity sheet*.

• Interview real people, including each other, or role played characters for news stories or broadcast magazine features.

• Record performances of scenes from any play or dramatisation. Get students producing edited versions with soundtracks and special effects, or edited highlights, or out-takes, or mini clips. On location or in the classroom.

• Get students recording each other's speaking and listening assessment activities, from which they can work on their own set of clips showing them at their best for assessment purposes, or highlighting the areas they need to work on some more.

### What's the point?

It's exciting for the technologically motivated, and for those who need to be up and doing. It's important that students learn something of how news and other media products are the product of editorial decisions, and being directly involved in those brings it home very clearly.

### Tricks of the trade

Make sure everyone gets off to a productive start by running through the basic operations of the camera. Deal with the excitement by having a funny five minutes where they can all film each other doing weird things with body parts, after which the focus is on the task.

### Variations on a theme

• To go the full monty, perhaps as part of a special curriculum enrichment session, set up a TV production simulation activity. Check out Channel 4's excellent set of materials and resources at **www.channel4.com >learning>breaking the news**.

### Whizzing it

It's all in the editing software. This doesn't need to be anything fancy or expensive, so if your school/college doesn't have a Media department, don't panic. Windows Movie Maker is a very simple little programme that comes bundled free in with Windows XP. It's not fancy but it does the basic job and using it is very intuitive (well, your students will probably think so, anyway…).

# Finger puppets

Don't mock it till you've tried it...

## The basic idea

Sticky gluey shiny spangly things. And/or a raid on the primary section of your school's educational supplies catalogue for some finger puppet templates, heads on sticks, or whatever. Personal faves are the cardboard people with two holes in the bottom to put your fingers through as legs. Paper plates and lolly sticks also work. Students make puppets and then work out a dramatised version of the text for performance to the rest of the class, younger students, a sell-out national tour.

## Applying it

• Try it with fairy tales, folk tales, Aesop's Fables, ballads, *The Canterbury Tales*.

• Check out the puppet show idea in Teachit's **Key Stage 3>Drama>A Midsummer Night's Dream (NLS Y8)>Tried and tested ideas**.

• Anything with ghosts or monsters to get students thinking carefully about how to represent these presences, and about how the author has done it.

• A lively technique for getting students to summarise what they consider to be the essence of the narrative: useful for consolidation after reading, for revision, or to engage students in close reading of shorter texts such as narrative poems.

## What's the point?

If it's good enough for Julie Andrews and the Von Trapp family kids, it's good enough for my class. But in case the rest of your team think you have actually cracked, it's also excellent for helping students to 'see' the essential components of the narrative and to understand plot. Designing the puppets requires a close focus on character and how much of the characterisation is or isn't about obvious physical qualities. Drama work is good for the soul, with students empathising with characters, working collaboratively, and exploring the dynamics of imagined situations. And if anyone is on your case about real world contexts for student work well, hey, turn it into a class 'Theatre in Education' project and you're away (you didn't want to do SATs preparation anyway, now did you?...)

## Tricks of the trade

If you want good discussion of characterisation you need to set the bar reasonably high for the standard of the puppets, getting them thinking about how to represent both internal and external qualities of the characters. Setting a time limit for the product, the dramatisation, gets students to focus more sharply on the key events and how they hang together as a plot. You need to set challenging expectations, and setting it up so that the performance is for other people is a useful way of doing this. Threatening to remove body parts is of course the other...

## Variations on a theme

• As a pre-reading task for a text with fairly archetypal characters and a strong moral scenario, give students the basic information and get them to devise their own narrative. Once you start reading, you will have lots of comparisons to discuss and they will be much better at seeing the text as the product of choices the writer has made and not a divinely ordained blob of literary stuff.

• To add some extra spice, give some students a particular interpretative angle to work on, e.g. a modern version of *The Wife of Bath* (à la BBC).

• Advanced students could be introduced to basic literary theory by getting each group to produce a version from a particular theoretical perspective, i.e. the feminist or Marxist or psychoanalytical finger puppet versions of *Hamlet*. This would present interesting choices to be made about interpretation of character and selection of key scenes.

• Writing reviews of each other's productions can encourage better concentration and critical evaluation during the performance.

• Another nice task is to get students to write a production log during the activity, with a concluding evaluation of their performance and what they have learned about the text by doing it.

## Whizzing it

Go all 'Aardman Animations' with a digital video camera and editing software. Who knows what creative talent might emerge!

# Flowcharts

Diagrams to represent plot processes at work

## The basic idea

Students use standard symbols to construct flowcharts representing processes at work in their text: actions, decisions, information, and consequences. Whole plots can be represented in chart form, with space for imaginative exploration of the decisions not taken and where these might have led.

## Applying it

• Useful for seeing the structure of long narrative poems as something that works between and beyond this stanza or that. Try it with Keats' 'Isabella, or The Pot of Basil' and see how much your students can improve the version on the next page.

• Works well with the big hitting Shakespeares like *Macbeth* and *Romeo and Juliet* – lots of striking actions and decisions, documents and information that are relatively simple to document in this format. Great for plot revision.

• The bigger the challenge you want to provide, the bigger the text to represent in this way. Jane Austen always a good option: try it with *Pride and Prejudice*. Give 'em a classic Victorian door-stopper and they'll be busy for hours…

• Get students using simple flow charts to model the ifs and ands of specific language features, as in Teachit's **Key Stage 3>Skills>Word level work – phonics, spelling and vocabulary>There, they're and their flow diagram**.

### What's the point?

It gets students to 'see' the plot structure. This requires careful and logical thinking about the key events, decisions, and information which shape

| | | | |
|---|---|---|---|
| (rounded rectangle) | **Start or End** | (parallelogram) | **Input or Output of information** |
| (rectangle) | **Action or Process** | (document shape) | **Document** |
| (diamond) | **Decision** | (D-shape) | **Delay** |
| (sub routine box) | **Sub routine e.g. sub plot** | → | **Flow line** |

the text. Representing them as a series of connected symbols involves the fine art of summarising. The exploration of alternative decisions and actions encourages speculative thinking, which may lead to rich imaginative work.

### Tricks of the trade

Make sure students understand the symbols first. Have a practice with a simple routine like getting to school in the morning. And it only works with texts where there is some kind of process at work, so those with lots of plot.

### Variations on a theme

• Instead of students drawing the shapes, they could use pre-prepared paper shapes so that they can tangibly play around with ideas before committing them to pen and ink in their books.

• Try it macro scale with the whole text, or micro scale with a key scene or chapter; or get different students working on different scales.

• Link to imaginative writing of alternative plot lines – the what if… Get them changing the shapes, changing the contents and seeing what diagram they end up with before writing the story.

### Whizzing it

There are standard shapes available in the flowchart section of the autoshapes menu on the drawing toolbar in Microsoft Word. If students enter 'draw a flowchart' into the search box of the Help menu, they'll find all the relevant information they could possibly need about connecting shapes, adding text and colours. Once they've done them, get a set of the shapes up on your IWB and have students moving them around to demonstrate their diagrams on the big screen.

## A flow chart of the plot processes at work in John Keats' 'Isabella, or the Pot of Basil'

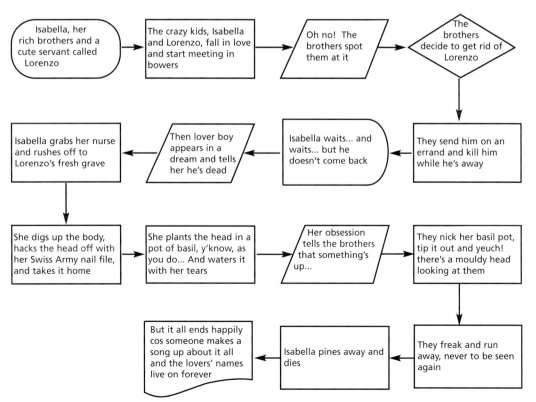

# Freeze frame

## Getting them to stand still for a second

## The basic idea

Students work out and present a tableau-like thing, a frozen moment of performance of a scene, a passage or a poem. The idea is that it will reveal significant ideas about character dynamics, emotions, and subtle detail that might be easier to see when nothing is moving.

## Applying it

- Get groups of students working on three short sections of *A Christmas Carol* with Teachit's **Key Stage 3> Prose>A Christmas Carol by Charles Dickens>Tableau activity 1-3**.

- For large-scale frozen action, pick moments from the play where there is a lot going on and have lots of students involved: the map scene in *King Lear* works well, as does the banquet scene in *Macbeth*. Build it up a few students at a time, with those waiting in the wings discussing who should go where and do what.

- Or have groups working on intimate moments: make your classroom Goths happy with all the deathbed scenes. The pile-up at the end of *Othello* is particularly good.

- Try it with poems, especially for bringing a bit of life to anthology work. For revision, allocate the poems in secret then have the rest of the class guess which is being shown and discuss whether or not the freeze frame has identified the most important aspects of the poem.

## What's the point?

Students have to read closely and carefully. The focus on a single moment encourages detailed thought and imaginative visualisation. It encourages a dramatic awareness of texts, with students having to think hard about maximising the potential for meaning of spatial relations, body language, and expression. Students who enjoy active performance work will have fun. The fact that it's a silent medium also makes it fun for teachers. Although they do have to discuss it before and after...

## Tricks of the trade

Let the students work out where they want to be and then count down as they move into their positions before saying 'Freeze!'. Make sure they have a clear grasp of what a frozen moment

should show, and the factors they will need to consider to do it well. Without movement or words, other aspects of performance come into play. If you have some budding thesps, spread them out amongst the groups to give them a useful leadership opportunity.

## Variations on a theme

- With a 'big' scene, try this. Students form pairs. Allocate roles to each pair. One of the pair will take part in the freeze frame, the other will be their coach, 'sculpting' them into position, helping them work out where they are going to stand, how and with what expression. You then direct a series of freeze frames from the scene: beginning, middle and end. The coaches make observations about what they see.

- You could give groups the same moment, different moments, or let them choose freely from the scene. Some moments are more challenging than others, so use this to differentiate for gifted readers and talented performers.

- Experiment by giving different focal points for the same moment; special focus on a particular character or the relationship between certain characters; or draw out the patterns of imagery in some way.

- Analytical discussion of each freeze frame is useful, but as an alternative, let students pick one of the characters in it and write an imaginative account of what they see, how they feel, etc in this moment. Nice...

## Whizzing it

Record on digital video so that students can watch it again, develop their analysis, use clips in presentations, and give you material for years to come, especially next time you do it and the students say 'You what, sir?' There's nothing quite like seeing your work up on the big screen to encourage more serious reflection on the quality of what you've done.

# Gained in translation

Old text into modern

## The basic idea

Help students get to grips with unfamiliar language forms by getting them 'translating' it into familiar ones. Most often used for texts written in pre-twentieth century English, but can also be used to 'translate' from one register or variety into another: formal to informal, jargon to plain English, standard English to dialect.

### Applying it

• Can be done as a simple matching exercise as in Teachit's *Key Stage 3/4>Drama>Macbeth-Act 3>Translate Shakespeare's words* where students match phrases in the Scottish play from Early Modern English into Modern English. For a more sophisticated task give students the Modern English and get them to find the matching quotation in the text, as in Teachit's *Key Stage 3>SATS> Macbeth Act 3>Act 3 Scene 4*. Or do it both ways!

• For a bigger fun/more creative approach to Shakespeare's use of language, get them playing around with two-way translation of lively expressions as in Teachit's *Key Stage 3/4>Drama>Introduction to Shakespeare: language> Shakespeare's language*.

• For even more creativity, get students turning speeches and soliloquies into vernacular speech. Try Hamlet's 'To be or not to be' for a contemporary twist on a classic expression of adolescent angst. Or update Dickensian caricatures as in Teachit's *Key Stage 3>Prose>Introducing Mr Dickens>Table 2: Caricatures*.

### What's the point?

In its simple forms, it helps students to recognise connections between older and newer forms of language, hopefully putting paid to the forlorn wailing of 'but it's in a foreign language sir'. In its richer forms, it gets students working with language, manipulating it directly so they can 'feel' those connections for themselves. It is excellent for the development of flexible thinking, encouraging an active problem solving approach to linguistic difficulty. The fact that it's challenging for most students is part of the point of doing it.

### Tricks of the trade

Set a challenging task and provide support for students who need it. There are all sorts of ways of doing this: you could give some students the matching task and some the full monty, but I prefer the subtler approach of making clues available as and when students need them as students can sometimes surprise you with their facility with this kind of task. If they are likely to depend on clues unnecessarily, give them some play money and make them 'buy' clues at an exorbitant rate that will require careful budgeting – and therefore harder thinking - to get through the task.

### Variations on a theme

• Get the Chaucer rapper, Baba Brinkman, into your school/college for a hiphop style *General Prologue*. Or buy the CD. More details at **http://aspirations.english.cam.ac. uk>*Converse>Chaucer4All***. Can't afford it? Get your students doing it for themselves (always a better idea anyway…).

### Whizzing it

Teachit's splendid resource on the General Prologue *Key Stage 3>Poetry>Canterbury Tales>Canterbury Tales Resource Pack (2 - while reading)* gets students turning sentences into Middle English using the 'Chaucer's postcards' tool on the same website as above: **http://aspirations.english.cam.ac.uk >*Converse >Chaucer4All >Teaching resources>Chaucer's postcards***. Hours of fun to be had there – and that's before you even get out of the staffroom…

# Game of chance

Dice throwing on types of question/comments

## The basic idea

Dice. Six types of information or question or topic area. Whatever number you roll is the type of question you have to answer or the kind of comment you have to make.

### Applying it

• In literary study, groups have a poem or short story or whatever. They read and annotate it for a while. Then they play with the dice. The six categories might be plot, themes, characterisation, settings, style, and genre. Whatever number they roll is what they have to talk about. If someone else has already commented on that, they have to elaborate, extend or challenge.

• For language study, have the sides of the dice representing word classes, and use to play a sentence building game, as in Teachit's **Key Stage 3>Skills>Lesson starters>Grammar dice**. Erm, also very useful for AS Language…

### What's the point?

This technique is not fancy, but it has novelty value during revision lessons, a feature much to be coveted in an otherwise deeply tedious part of the academic year. At other times it works to constrain student comments in productive ways, forcing them to find something to say about an aspect of the text they are less comfortable with, whereas in open discussion they can play to their existing strengths. Taking students a little way out of their comfort zone is always a good thing for learning.

### Tricks of the trade

Keep it snappy. Play for a short focused time otherwise the fivers will start coming out on the desk as students invent new gambling games to play. Follow it up with a period in which students review what comments were made and draw them together into a written or spoken presentation of some kind. Without that purpose it's just a bit of random dice throwing.

### Variations on a theme

• Get those role-playing game dice with seventeen sides (available from all good toy shops and/or Maths teachers), and see what your students make of that! Get them to invent relevant categories of information.

• For straightforward revision purposes, build it up into a full blown Trivial Pursuit type game, only not trivial, obviously.

# Game design

Board/computer game based on text or issues

## The basic idea

Students take a text, a topic or their own fertile imagination and, well, design a game to play based on it. A board game of their own confection, or based on an existing model, such as snakes and ladders. Or a computer game based on some kind of quest scenario. They produce the whole thing, including the instructions, cheat sheets, even a promotional campaign to sell their game if you want to milk it to the max.

### Applying it

• Produce a board game version of *Oliver Twist* with Teachit's **Key Stage 3>Prose>Oliver Twist by Charles Dickens>Board Game**. Includes beautifully developed instructions. Now that is nice...

• Similarly, for Robin Hood legends generally, or specifically Tony Robinson's *Maid Marian and her Merry Men*, try Teachit's **Key Stage 3>Drama>Maid Marian and her Merry Men>Design a board game and wordsearch**. I want the Friar Tuck counter, okay?

• For a generic snake and ladders game template that can be used to design a game to go with any narrative, check out Teachit's **Key Stage 3/4>Skills> Reading skills>Snakes and ladders**.

• Try it with an issue like youth homelessness. Get them researching and reading case studies and stories, charity leaflets and poems. Then they produce a board game that takes a player through some of the experiences.

• Works well with that perennially popular list of ages at which young people can legally do certain things. Snakes and ladders-type game in which full legally recognised adulthood is the target.

• Oxfam has a nice board game design project for Key Stage 1 on sustainability, but this is entirely adaptable to other key stages – just up the ante on the reading material. See **www.oxfam.org.uk/ coolplanet> Resources>Free online teaching materials> Sustainability>Global citizenship> Key stage 1**.

*(continued over)*

## What's the point?

Like so many engaging activities one of its primary purposes is to develop closer reading, and this does the trick. Students have to be highly selective, encouraging fine discrimination, judgement and much debate. It is creative in the way it gets students working with knowledge in a hands on way, it gives group work a meaningful focus, and for students who like to do it it's a lesson from heaven. Snakes and ladders is a particularly good format as it focuses attention on the ups and downs of life situations, real or fictional. This can be very powerful in developing empathy and worldly awareness. Also brilliant for getting students to do real instructional writing without them even knowing they're doing it.

## Tricks of the trade

Pick your application carefully. You need a text or a topic where there are lots of possibilities, both in terms of game format and potential content. If it's all a bit clear cut it won't be any fun. Then make sure you have the resources to make games they actually want to play with afterwards. An A3 sheet of paper and a biro is okay, but oh, plundering the educational supplies catalogue, raiding your Art or D&T department under cover of darkness, or kidnapping those teachers to help you is so much more inspiring. For full on motivation, get the students creating the games to play with prospective pupils at the next open evening.

## Variations on a theme

• If the thought of all those scissors flying around your classroom leaves you stone cold, try playing games other people have made. Try Captain Campaign here: **www.demgames.org/leeds**.

• Proprietary board games based on TV series can also be a good starting point if you can get enough of them for a pound in the charity shop, or enough students to donate their unwanted Christmas presents. Try *Doctor Who* games, *Buffy the Vampire Slayer* games, etc. They are generally rubbish. So get the students producing a better science fiction, or vampire, or whatever game. Then get them to write the narrative. Hours of productive storytelling work.

• If you've got £100 to spend, your class can design and have manufactured your very own Monopoly game that comes in a dead cool tin box. And even if you haven't, they helpfully provide all the resources for you to do the teacher's cheap DIY with a colour photocopier version at **http://uk.mymonopoly.com**.

• Send them off with their game and its instructions to road test on friends and relatives. Great for real redrafting work.

## Whizzing it

'Sir…Miss…why can't we do it on computers? It'd be loads better. This cardboard stuff is pants.'

'You can.'

Design tools, colours, fonts and unlimited possibilities. Or if you haven't got three weeks, set up a template that they can fill in.

# Goldfish bowl

Participants and observers

## The basic idea

Most students form a circle. They are the observers. In the middle a few students perform an activity or process of some sort. When they have finished, the observers either outline the process they have learned about by watching closely, or they give constructive feedback about the quality of the activity.

### Applying it

• A few students perform their version of a scene with everyone watching it 'in the round' and then giving feedback and suggestions.

• To develop instructional writing, get the student(s) in the middle to perform an interesting task of a complexity suited to the class. Works nicely if you get a student volunteer to demonstrate something to do with one of their hobbies. Observers have to note the process. They can then ask questions to clarify, etc, and away you go.

• For a productive speaking and listening assessment, have an equal number of observers and observed, with observers making notes on individuals according to the set criteria BUT having to stick to 'positive' or 'constructive' comments.

### What's the point?

It encourages a close whole class focus on a phenomenon. It can create a much more focused dynamic than sitting behind desks watching something happening at the front of the classroom because everyone is equidistant from the action and somehow the physical act of standing up makes them more involved.

### Tricks of the trade

Apart from the general principle of making sure what is happening in the middle is not a great big yawn, the main trick is to ensure the observers have precise things to focus on. Just watching can lead to drifting off and mucking about. Clipboards and observation schedules work well, with lots of opportunity to tick when things happen if you have very short attention spans to deal with. Always debrief the participants in the middle, giving them a brief opportunity to say how their life as a goldfish felt.

### Variations on a theme

• Get someone in to demonstrate something cool, a bit like in *The Generation Game* of yesteryear. Someone from the armed forces to show them how to assemble a big gun; a chef to ice a cake; or whatever will rock their boats (especially if they get to have a go too).

• If working on performances in this way, give observers the opportunity to freeze the scene, suggest ideas and improvements, then give the players a chance to try these out. You need confident performers to do this, but if you've got 'em, let 'em flaunt it!

# Graphs and charts
Plotting with a purpose

## The basic idea

Students create line graphs to give a visual representation of the emotional structure of the text. Make judgements about the degree of emotional intensity in a scene or section and plot how this goes up and down in the text. General emotional intensity, or specific named emotions. Make the y axis degrees of intensity and the x axis the chapter or scene numbers. Then students discuss what is most interesting about their graphs or charts.

## Applying it

• Degree of scariness in any horror or ghost story raises interesting discussion of different ideas about what constitutes scariness. Or plot tension against chapter numbers as in Teachit's **Key Stage 3>Prose> Abomination by Robert Swindells> Understanding tension in the novel.**

• Plot a contrasting pair of emotions during the course of a novel for a more complex task. Try it with hope and fear in *1984*.

• Take it a stage further by plotting multiple emotions. One line might represent how humour goes up and down in the play, another anger, another fear, or whatever. Either give each group one emotion to work on, and then combine everyone's efforts to explore comparisons, or get some or all of the groups to produce graphs with multiple lines.

• Try plotting a value against time to explore the plot structure, such as hope and time as in Teachit's **Key Stage 3>Prose>Two Weeks with the Queen by Morris Gleitzman> Hope versus time**. Or feelings against time as in **Key Stage 3>Drama>Macbeth – Act 3>The change in Macbeth's feelings during the play**.

• General intensity plotting works really well for any Shakespeare play, but best with the emotional rollercoasters.

## What's the point?

It helps students 'see' structural elements of the text, sorting out the wood from the trees. To plot the graph or chart students have to read closely, compare scenes or sections of the text carefully, and make judgements. Some of this will be as touchy-feely as the next activity, and very nice indeed for

your students with a high E.Q., but where it involves a nice bit of page counting, your students who are more comfortable with objective and measurable forms of knowledge will be happily occupied for a while. Plotting line graphs encourages discussion and debate about interpretation of intensity, and when it emerges as a finished product, much discussion can be had of the ebbs and flows in the structure of the text.

## Tricks of the trade

Think carefully about the constitution of the groups for this activity – share the mathematically astute around! If it's a bit daunting for your students to work with the whole text, you could pre-select a representative series of key speeches or passages for them to work with instead.

## Variations on a theme

• Instead of looking at the emotional or narrative structure of a whole text, try focusing in on a speech or a scene.

• In novels with multiple narration use bar charts or pie charts to show who gets what share of the narrative when. Try it with *Wuthering Heights*. Has also worked really well in teaching Matthew Kneale's *English Passengers* as an A2 coursework text.

• Use the graph to select the scene or section the student finds most interesting, or powerful, or moving, or scary, for detailed analysis of its mood and how this is conveyed by the writer.

## Whizzing it

Get them plotting their graphs and charts in electronic format. If you have different students working on different graphs, get them to collate it using a PC, then whack the projector on so that you can all look at the outcome on the big screen.

# Guided tours

Imagining self into a situation

## The basic idea

Take a situation that is way outside the realms of student experience, at least on the surface. Something they need to develop an empathy with in order to understand language, or a character, or a situation, or a process. Students close their eyes. You wait for them to get comfortable with the silence and the strangeness of this. Then you guide them through an imaginary landscape, giving them details of things they can see or hear, actions they are taking, places they are visiting, people they are meeting. Give time between each detail to shape it in their own imaginations.

Guide them right through to the situation at the heart of what you want them to understand, and then invite them to open their eyes and write down, without saying a word to anyone first, how it feels to be in this situation, the questions in their minds, the things they want to say or do – whatever. Let them write for as long as it takes, within the bounds of reason and good classroom management. Use this as the basis of discussion.

### Applying it

• A guided fantasy about the experience of slavery worked wonders time and again with waspish students needing to develop a more sophisticated understanding of the language of Grace Nichols, and in the wider context of language study at AS/A2.

• A guided fantasy about becoming ruler of the world brought out more sensitive and sophisticated ideas about utopia than had been managed previously in open brainstorming for this area of literary study.

• Also good for getting students to engage with a variety of settings. All the NATE Drama Packs have great Guided Tours – for *His Dark Materials*, *Rabbit-Proof Fence*, *Macbeth*, *Holes*, *Much Ado About Nothing*, *Anthology* (Different Cultures poems) and *Starseeker* - which take an active approach to this idea.

### What's the point?

The point is to relax the mind a bit, to let ideas flow without the need to shape them too much into conscious thoughts. Really creative ideas can emerge from this. It is completely and intentionally speculative and subjective so whatever students come up with is a positive contribution. It allows every student their own mental space to work in for a while, if only for a few minutes, without being crowded by other people's opinions and ideas. Learning to create that space is a powerful lesson for life quite apart from any value it has to the study of English. It's also a sort of dramatic recreation without having to do any of that scary acting stuff.

### Tricks of the trade

The whole eyes shut and silence thing can be a level of challenge beyond some students and you need to judge this carefully before deciding to use this technique. It may be a matter of quiet persistence on your part, or of rearranging students in different seating

patterns before you start, or of keeping it very short the first time you do it. If it starts bombing, don't shout or shush too much or it destroys the magic, just quietly withdraw at an earlier stage and use the rest of the scenario as a straightforward role-play.

Always debrief the activity before looking at its products by asking the simple question, 'How did it feel to do that?' When everyone's back in reality, explore the ideas generated. Sometimes this activity produces very powerful emotional stuff, so it can be best to ask students what they want to share with the group rather than making them read out everything they've written. You need to be careful not to go too deeply into strong memories. Powerful recall has the power to cause intense emotional upset with very responsive students. Go gently to start with and see what comes out.

### Variations on a theme

• If students were just getting somewhere when you stopped them and made them talk about it, they might like to write the full story.

• For a creative way into writing poetry, guide students gently into a room/space of their choosing but pause regularly for them to write down one directed line of a poem focused on a smell/touch/sound/thought/ emotion. The final collection of lines will form the basis for a poem which will need shaping and filling out. Amazing what happens when you only have to write one line at a time.

# Half-baked ideas

Tinkering around with stuff to make it better

## The basic idea

Take some information that is not quite what your students need. Instead of you spending time researching and rewriting it, transforming it into a tidy handout or PowerPoint, get your students to do it.

## Applying it

- There are all kinds of guidelines for writing book reviews. Have students soup them up, varying them for different age groups, and getting friends, relatives, significant others reviewing as many books as possible for World Book Day.

- Instead of giving students a model A grade answer in exam preparation, give them a C or D grade essay and get them to improve it. Or give different students differently graded work so that they work on an appropriate improvement level.

- Spoof 'how to' guidelines make this a fun activity. Check these spoof instructions for Australian TV drama and bestselling epic fantasy novel **http://members.ozemail.com.au/~i mcfadyen >Not the Net>Famous Writers School**. Entertaining, with some useful kernels of truth, which we laughed at, questioned, then turned into a serious set of guidelines before having a go at the writing.

- Instead of giving critical statements about the text the Ten Commandments treatment, get students to modify them. Teachit's *Key Stage 5>Prose>Captain Corelli's Mandolin by Louis de Bernières>The exorbitant auditory impediment* invites this kind of approach with a series of half-baked critical statements made by other students about a section of *Captain Corelli's Mandolin*.

- Also works well as a reverse kind of brainstorming or the second part of the brainstorming activity, in which students are given a muddle of half-baked ideas about a topic and invited to eliminate what is not useful, refine the things that are, and add any extra ingredients needed.

## What's the point?

It halves your preparation time and triples the amount of learning that takes place. Too often in our desire to make knowledge accessible we do all the work and consequently we have all the learning. On top of that, in giving students the ready meal, we are not teaching them to handle the raw ingredients, and if they are to become successful independent learners, we must. Knowledge is not tidy.

### Tricks of the trade

The resource needs to be sufficiently useful and intriguing that it's worth bothering with; it can't just be any old random piece of web-rubbish. It's also a technique to build up steadily if you are working in a context where students are used to having everything dished up on a plate for them. Otherwise you get 'why don't you just tell us' type questions. Start with simple statements for modification and build upwards until students are used to being more creative in their thinking.

### Variations on a theme

- Give students a story and get them to improve it. Though they might be a little daunted by tackling Dickens, popular ephemeral fiction as in women's magazines can be a rich source (especially when boys add in gun-toting episodes and some vampires/zombies and improve the genre immeasurably).

### Whizzing it

Anything that involves modifying text is more easily done with word processing tools. Use the tracking feature in Word and students will more easily be able to develop a commentary on what they have changed and why. This is a much more useful and realistic approach to drafting than working from the outdated mental model of distinct and separate draft documents.

# Hangman

My exciting Christmas special

## The basic idea

Yeah, yeah, we all know how to play this, don't we? Have a word or phrase outlined in blank spaces on the board. Students guess a letter. If it occurs in the word you write it in as many times as it occurs. If it doesn't, you start drawing a gallows. The aim is for the students to correctly identify the word before they are 'hung'. If that's a bit gruesome, just give them a number of lives that get crossed off – nine is always a good number and gives students cats to think about instead…

### Applying it

• Cheap and easy revision task where terminology is important. Soup it up a bit by giving bonus points or spot prizes if they can also illustrate it with an example, and explain it.

• I've used it a few times when I've become fed up with seeing the same basic spelling errors time and time again in most students' work. In evil teacher mode we play the nice, fun, easy game, and then I make them learn all the spellings for a test. At key stage 5…

### What's the point?

It's nothing fancy, but it can get students to focus a bit more sharply on key words. It's also an important survival strategy to have techniques for taking your foot off the accelerator once in a while without anyone really noticing. A bit lame in other respects, yes, but useful for a moment of freewheeling: almost no preparation, and none if you set it up so that whoever guesses the word sets the next one.

### Tricks of the trade

Keeping everyone engaged is the key trick, although the simple opportunity to play a game in class will carry you a long way in the classroom goodwill stakes in many contexts. Try pitting teams against each other. Try pitting pairs of students against each other in a series of rounds. Try winner stays on. Let them test you on terminology.

### Variations on a theme

• Go more like *Wheel of Fortune* with the size of the phrases and use it to get students focusing on key quotations that are short and pithy. Let them use their books if that's too hard at first but, if they have closed book exams to sit, build up to a point where they can do it without.

• Instead of playing it with lots of words, use it as a starter to recap a key concept or word or useful framing quotations from last lesson.

### Whizzing it

Set it up in Word to go on the interactive whiteboard. Have your word blanks in place. Have the letters of the alphabet in layered text boxes so that you have a pile of As, a pile of Bs, etc. Then you can drag and drop the letters into place when they are correctly guessed. Give students a go at being quizmaster too, especially if they might otherwise be distracted.

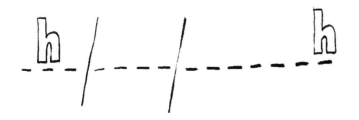

# Headlining

Adding the chapter/section/scene titles the publishers obviously forgot

## The basic idea

Take a novel, a play, a long short story or a narrative poem. Divide into appropriate sections if chapter, scene or section numbers don't exist. Then students give each one a heading that pithily captures the essence of the section. This can be played straight as in Hardy's *Far From the Madding Crowd*, e.g. '2. Night – the flock – an interior – another interior'. Or get them writing more creative headlines. Try tabloid style for memorability; compact broadsheet style for textual dignity. Students write their headlines onto their copy (or post-it notes to stick into their copy) of the text for future reference purposes.

### Applying it

- Supply or customise chapter headlines in any long novel (okay, so *Great Expectations* is one of Dickens' shorter efforts, but all things are relative, and relative to *Hello*! that's long...), and even in some shorter ones. Change the prime number chapter headings in *The Curious Incident of the Dog in the Night-time* by Mark Haddon to verbal ones (and explore what's with the number ones while you're at it...)

- Scene and act headlines for just about any Shakespeare play but especially those with the more complex twists and turns, disguises and deceptions, plots and subplots. I love doing these lurid tabloid style. Don't ask me why...

- Explore what students see as the most important elements with section headings for long poems like 'The Lady of Shalott' or 'The Rime of the Ancient Mariner'.

- Show pre-twentieth century novels that make elaborate use of chapter headings in their contents pages, such as in Dickens' *Nicholas Nickleby*, e.g. '6. In which the Occurrence of the Accident mentioned in the last Chapter, affords an opportunity to a couple of Gentlemen to tell Stories against each other.' Do it in this style with a modern novel.

### What's the point?

On a basic level, it helps students remember what's where in a text so that with a long text they have some hope of finding it again. You can see immediately if there are gaps in a student's understanding of the section and/or if they have unearthed a really interesting original angle on it. It is also a cunning way of finding out who has done the independent reading of the text you set: no headline, no tick in your mark book. Er, and with the one-tick school of marking, you get a night off to read a novel yourself – hurrah! And on top of all that, it can build summary skills, creativity with language, and lay useful foundations for future work on plot structure.

### Tricks of the trade

Get students to do it as they go along in the reading. If you try doing it all at the end, they will understandably get headline fatigue and produce lame efforts. Try having spot prizes each week for the best headlines: often it's the students you least expect who produce the most interesting, especially if they are avid tabloid readers.

### Variations on a theme

- Combine with poster activity to produce, as a class, a complete visual summary of the text. Very useful way of 'seeing' the plot.

- Set the headline challenge: to read the section(s) or chapter(s) needed and produce the best headline to be voted on by the class. Or collect and collate headlines produced. Then students to pick one they disagree with and write a paragraph arguing their case against it – good reverse thinking.

### Whizzing it

Collect the headlines produced and pick one for each chapter or section. Where possible, pick one from each student. Put them into text boxes. Mix them up. There you go, one nice activity to start work on plot or for revision – students use PCs or the IWB to sort them into the right order.

# Highlighter heaven

Fun with fluorescent pens

## The basic idea

Get a load of packs of highlighter pens from the stationery lair. Photocopies of a text. Colour coding a-go-go according to what it is you want students to focus on. Nice and easy.

### Applying it

- Take a scene from a play or a chapter or whatever. Have students highlighting in one colour the most significant or powerful line or sentence, the second most significant in another, the third another. Use to explore structure.

- Useful for all kinds of language feature spotting as a way into richer discussion of function and effect. Teachit's resource **Key Stage 3>Skills>Sentence level work – grammar and punctuation> Reference chains** gets students highlighting features of textual cohesion.

- Try highlighting all the adjectives in a text before exploring what they are doing there. For a text extract that has already been done for you try Teachit's **Key Stage 3>Prose> Introducing Mr Dickens>Extract 1a (1) Dotheboys Hall**.

- Colour code an anthology of poems to show connections of theme, tone, style, etc. Trashes the book but good for revision.

- For a colour coding activity to help develop approaches to essay writing, check out Teachit's **Key Stage 4>Prose>Of Mice and Men by John Steinbeck>Animals and other creatures in Of Mice and Men**. Students give a series of key points one of five colours; five key points go with each colour; before you know it, you've got a detailed essay plan that can be debated, modified, exemplified – er, and maybe even written....

- Colour code a pool of adjectives to identify which ones go with which character as in Teachit's **Key Stage 4>Drama>An Inspector Calls by J.B. Priestley>Describing character**.

### What's the point?

It gets students focusing on specific details and colour coding can be a powerful visual stimulus to memory. It demands active engagement with the text and commitment to an answer.

### Tricks of the trade

Have enough pens! It's also a good idea to have spare copies of the poem as someone will get in a muddle at some point. If you have a lot of students with an over-anxiety about 'spoiling their work' you might get less stress if you do this using ICT, as students can correct their work and print it out and it still looks pretty. However, such prettification is not always a good thing to encourage, whereas creative mess is. It's about the learning not about the colours…

### Variations on a theme

- You can get students each looking at several issues with several different colours. Or you can get different students each looking at one thing with one colour. Then group them so that they combine on one master document. Either is good, but each slightly different in dynamics. The more group work involved in this, the better the opportunities for differentiation – either naturally occurring or facilitated through the different challenges you set individuals.

- Get students to highlight all the words they like best in a poem or passage, or find most moving or powerful. Get them to write these down in a list. Then if it was a poem they started with, they write a paragraph or two of description or story - or if a passage of prose they had, a poem – using all of these words. Explore what happens, then see what they have to say about the original text.

### Whizzing it

An ideal opportunity for full technicolour multimedia glory on PCs or interactive whiteboard. Use change of font colour or shading tool to highlight.

# Hole filling
## Creative insertions

## The basic idea

Take one text that has at least one curious hole in it. The kind of hole that your bright but oh-I-wish-you-hadn't-just-asked-me-that student will always find. Without fail. Instead of fighting the creeping sense of doom that you will never finish the syllabus, embrace the creative chaos and get students filling in the hole with speculative discussion and imaginative writing. Suddenly you'll find the syllabus is finished after all.

### Applying it

- How come Robinson Crusoe only found one footprint when Friday appears to have had two legs?

- What is all that about Lady Macbeth's babies?

- What did Heathcliff do in his Gap Year?

- What happened to Othello on his voyage to Cyprus?

- Any suitable options from John Sutherland's books of literary detective puzzles: *Is Heathcliff a Murderer?* and *Can Jane Eyre Be Happy?*

- Insert a scene that is referred to but not developed as in Teachit's **Key Stage 4>Drama>Whose life is it anyway? by Brian Clark>Writing an extra scene**.

### What's the point?

It gets students reading closely and carefully between the lines of a text. It can lead to really interesting exploration of the idea that as much is said by the silences as by the words, and intriguing alternative interpretations of the text start opening up. Speculation encourages creative thinking, discussion tends to be animated, and encouraging imaginative responses to the text creates space for students to engage with it in their own way.

### Tricks of the trade

Choose holes or mysteries that are really intriguing, not ones with an obvious answer. Unless your purpose is only really about stimulating creative writing, make sure you do a debrief afterwards to bring students back to the reality of the text as it has been published. Useful questions might include, 'What did the writer actually do with this section?', 'What meaning(s)/effect(s) do these choices produce?', 'What have you learned from imagining what happens in the spaces in the text?' Otherwise expect some really weird exam answers…

### Variations on a theme

- Challenge some students to write in the style of the author, create a revised edition of the text, and use that to explore what difference the added chapter or section makes. Great for understanding texts as the product of choices made by writers.

- The leisurely version will involve finding the hole, exploring it through discussion, and all the stages of good imaginative writing development. The speedy version might focus only on the speculative discussion as a lead-in to fuller discussion of different ways of interpreting the text.

- Insert a 'missing' character. Works really well with the *General Prologue to the Canterbury Tales*, with students working from a list of authentic medieval occupations.

### Whizzing it

Get them publishing their stories on a fan fiction website and they should get published acclaim and reviews from other readers. Motivating stuff.

# Hotseating

Putting a character in the hot seat - or the electric chair

## The basic idea

One student becomes one of the characters from a text, fictional or non-fictional, or its author. Other students ask him/her questions in role: about events in the text, motivation, relationships with other characters, biographical background. The student in role draws on his/her detailed knowledge of the text, as well as elaborating, extemporising, and good old-fashioned spontaneous invention of a viable and credible story, also known as 'blagging'. The other essential skill of hamming it up in a good cause is also to be encouraged.

### Applying it

• The hot seat doesn't come much hotter than Frankie waiting in the chair in the ballad of 'Frankie and Johnny'. What will her take on the events be as she awaits her death?

• Hotseating 'good' characters can be a bit Richard and Judy, so for the bad guys think about using something more like the patented Jack Bauer approach to discovering what a character really really thinks... Get Mrs Coulthard (and her monkey) from *Northern Lights* in the hot seat for a bit of a grilling. And that Richard III bloke...

• Works well with any terminally confused character. Hamlet... Pip from *Great Expectations*...

• Cordelia's decision to do that whole 'nothing' thing largely makes me want to slap her. High time she was put in the hot seat, just before she dies, to justify her actions. Try Iago on what exactly his problem is, and Frankenstein on why he couldn't just go to Biology lessons like everybody else.

### What's the point?

For the person in the hot seat, it encourages imaginative engagement and empathy with another person, and a sense of telling their life's story between and beyond the text. For the interlocutors, it encourages good questioning as a form of enquiry. For both, it can tease out ideas about what the writer did or didn't choose to include, and the significance of silences.

### Tricks of the trade

It's all about which student goes into the hot seat. Choose the most charismatic students who will do the homework on the figure in question, and be able to respond imaginatively and spontaneously. Those with high emotional intelligence and good oral skills generally do a better job than those who understand every nuance of the text. The other trick lies in the preparation of the other students. Leaving questioning to chance is not as effective as getting the student to prepare at least one opening question. And always always always debrief the student who was in the hot seat with a 'how was it for you' question.

### Variations on a theme

• Ask your favourite Performing Arts students to be in the hot seat for younger children if you want the focus to be on the accuracy of the information given. Dressing up? Why not?...

• Instead of doing this in a whole class format, break it down into smaller groups so that more students can be in the hot seat. Different groups could all work on the same character and compare ideas, or on different characters and pool ideas.

• Use this as the foundation for writing imaginative dramatic monologues.

• Instead of doing it yourself, study the masters at work out there in the real world, especially for language study: Paxman on *Newsnight*; Humphreys on the *Today* programme, a couple of shock jock talk DJs. See what else the students can find.

# Illustrated editions

## Exploring through drawing

## The basic idea

Students produce an illustrated edition of the text or part of the text. Original images they create themselves, comic strips, or found images from books, magazines, art galleries, Google, etc. Give them a fixed number of images allowed, and let them decide which aspects of the text to illustrate.

## Applying it

• Produce a comic strip version of Jaque's speech about the seven ages of man in *As You Like It*. Example in Teachit's **Key Stage 3>Drama> Introduction to Shakespeare: the plays>All the world's a stage...comic strip!**

• Illustrate individual poems, as in Teachit's **Key Stage 3>Poetry>The deserted house>A copy of the poem with activities**. Build up into an illustrated anthology as in **Key Stage 3>Poetry>War poetry>A 13 page lesson pack**

• Produce ten appropriately terrifying images to illustrate a new 'Nightmares in Literature' edition of Coleridge's 'Rime of the Ancient Mariner'.

• Illustrate a soliloquy to explore the use of imagery: try *Macbeth* and the dagger soliloquy. Or illustrate Banquo's description of the witches using Teachit's **Key Stage 3>Drama>Macbeth – Act 1>Act 1 Scene 3 – the three witches**.

• Focus on key episodes in a long novel after the hard slog through the reading. Nine illustrations to appear in a schools edition of *Tess of the D'Urbervilles*.

• Also works well with narrative poems and AS/A2 students. Six illustrations each for 'Isabella', 'Eve of St Agnes' and 'Lamia' for a sumptuous new edition of Keats' longer poems.

## What's the point?

It can encourage careful thinking about which aspects of the text are the most significant, and detailed re-reading of these passages to help visualise the scene for the reader. Visualisation tasks get students committing to an interpretation of the text, and these interpretations can be much more easily discussed and compared. It can also give a much needed bit of breathing space from time to time.

## Tricks of the trade

Have interesting creative resources for all students to work with, but allow for different levels of artistic skill by having a good variety available, including magazines (not battered ripped up ones that nobody in their right mind would want to touch) for straightforward image finding for the artistically challenged. The task can be done individually or collectively. The latter encourages more debate, but realistically you do end up with one person doing the art work and everyone else watching. So, for once, I usually favour individual work on this.

## Variations on a theme

• Either as the main activity, or as an extra level of challenge for some students, give different instructions about the type of edition of the text to be illustrated. To speed it up, slow it down, or provide different types and levels of challenge, vary the number of images required.

• Do it in reverse by exploring the images artists have produced of key scenes in literary texts. Try Fuseli's 'King Lear Supported by Kent and the Fool', or Blake's 'Lear and Cordelia in Prison', or Runciman's 'The Three Witches'. These and many more available in the Tate's exhibition catalogue *Gothic Nightmares*.

## Whizzing it

With a relatively short text that is available as an e-text, get students scanning in their images, inserting them in the right place, and saving as their own personal edition of the text. Use the digital image files on the big screen to showcase and compare interpretations by different students.

# Imitation

Flattery and parody

## The basic idea

Students explore the style of an author, poet or dramatist – or a speech writer, or a particular genre – and then write their own piece in the same style, either with serious intent or to parody, as they choose.

### Applying it

• Study the language and style of Chaucer in the *General Prologue*, and then get students writing 'missing pilgrim' portraits.

• Parodies of William Carlos Williams' poem 'This Is Just To Say' abound, and are excellent for exploring just what Williams is up to and what poetry is or should be. Check here for further resources: **www.favoritepoem.org >Poems> Variations on a theme by William Carlos Williams**.

• Having a stab at Beowulf and/or Old English? Then you must check out Grendel's dog at **http://homepage.mac.com/mseffie >Assignments>Beowulf>Beocat**. Really good playing around with Old English word formations.

• In the unlucky years that Valentine's Day falls in term time, try a parody of Burns' 'A Red, Red Rose' before reading Shakespeare's 'Sonnet 130' in the AQA anthology.

### What's the point?

The opportunity to send up a text is one students delight in, and they engage enthusiastically in it without realising how much they are learning about language and style. That's got to be a result in anyone's book.

### Tricks of the trade

Don't expect students to know what a parody is. Guide them into it with an example and have a bit of a look at how it works, in literature and/or popular culture. Then unleash them. If they need formal knowledge about the writer's language and style at the end of it, make sure you spend time after the fun of writing in teasing it out as students can often produce fantastic parodies intuitively without being any better able to write about language, structure and form in an exam.

### Variations on a theme

• Instead of writing them, just read and explore. Lots of examples, ideas and inspiration in the *Faber Book of Parodies* edited by Simon Brett ISBN 0 57113254 5. Put it on your wish list and flash subliminally on the big screen every time they're innocuously watching a DVD...

• Parody Hollywood action movie trailers in writing summaries of the set text you have just read.

# Improvisation

Making stuff up and acting it out

## The basic idea

Students are given a basic outline of some characters and/or a scenario. They spontaneously make up a drama, inventing and developing the storyline as they go along. This may lead into rehearsed or scripted work later. It is different from role play in its creative freedom to go wherever the students take it.

## Applying it

- Host your very own murder mystery party with students improvising a character and his/her responses to the scenario. Try it with Teachit's **Key Stage 3>Drama>Murder mystery drama unit>Scheme of work**.

- As a pre-reading exercise, give students the raw scenario of the play e.g. for *King Lear*, a father has three daughters, he wants to share out his business and his wealth between them in exchange for a life of leisure. What happens? For a very nicely structured example for younger students see Teachit's **Key Stage 3>Drama>Much Ado About Nothing>Much Ado introductory activities**.

- Works well with any moral dilemma you/they can handle emotionally. Judge carefully your own limits as well as theirs...

- As an in-reading exercise, get students to improvise alternative storylines e.g. for *Wuthering Heights*, what might have happened had Cathy and Heathcliff done the quite obviously right thing and run away together?

## What's the point?

Students get a welcome bit of freedom to exercise their imagination in a playful non-committal kind of way. They will undoubtedly talk a lot, they will probablytry lots of ideas out, and if you have created the right kind of environment they may be lucky enough to experience the richly rewarding state of flow, where time and assessment objectives disappear and being in that moment is all that matters. And it gets them on the inside of a text looking out, instead of always being stuck on the outside looking in, like some Dickensian waif at the window.

## Tricks of the trade

Set a time limit with enough time for all of the groups either to perform their work or to give a formal presentation of the ideas they explored in their improvisation (the acceptable cop-out for those who would rather stand there and argue with you for a week than be seen dead performing in front of the class). Encourage comparative discussion of the different ideas that were created to bring out the most learning from the activity and avoid accusations of airy-fairiness.

### Variations on a theme

- To extend it, link to scripted and/or more fully rehearsed performances, or to imaginative written work based on the improvised ideas.

- Follow up with reading of the scene or passage the original scenario was drawn from, and develop comparative discussion of their own ideas with those of the writer.

- Give students a series of objects and get them to improvise a drama that involves references to all of them. These could be the objects that appear in a story you are going to read later. Or use a work of art as the starting point for creative improvisation of ideas for later narrative writing.

### Whizzing it

Get students rehearsing and recording a 'finished product' audio version of their narratives, complete with whatever digital bells and whistles they can dream up. Then podcast them to the world.

# Intercutting

Cutting and pasting for creative enlightenment

## The basic idea

Take a series of passages, poems or scenes – from the same text, the same writer, from the same genre, the same anthology, the same theme – whatever combination you can think of. Give students two such texts, with the invitation to chop them up into chunks (not individual words) and intercut the pieces. The point is to create a new text that is rich in imaginative suggestion and illuminates one or other or both texts in some way.

### Applying it

- Intercutting the opening scene and the closing scene is a good way of exploring how much is prefigured.

- Two scenes or speeches from a play. Try Hamlet and his women: take his big scene with Gertrude and his big scene with Ophelia. What happens when they are intercut?

- Works well with two poems. Interesting things always happen with 'The Passionate Shepherd to his Love' by Marlowe and 'Come. And Be My Baby' by Maya Angelou.

- Try it with different forms. What happens if you intercut WW1 poems?

### What's the point?

It gets students making connections and comparisons in much freer and more creative ways than straightforward compare and contrast jobs. It generates new literary texts, and these are often powerful and beautiful, making it a rewarding task to do with students who don't see themselves as good writers. Done collaboratively, there is much lively discussion about what should go where and why, opening a rich vein of interpretative comment to mine afterwards.

### Tricks of the trade

Choose sets of texts where you don't know what is going to happen or how it might turn out – makes it much more fun! Other than that, just watch out for flying scissors and have some spares if you're doing it the *Blue Peter* way in case the text gets minced, accidentally or otherwise.

### Variations on a theme

- For more challenge, have students intercutting a larger range of texts or longer texts. For less or to speed it up, give students the pieces rather than letting them decide.

- Get students choosing their own pair or trio of texts to be intercut from an anthology. Livens it up no end and beats filling in a comparison grid any day of the week.

- If you have enough time and/or copies, get students to produce two or three variations from the same texts, then explore how each constructs different meanings and interpretations.

### Whizzing it

Have the texts available in Word form on the network so cutting and pasting can be done without the need for flying scissors.

# Interviewing

Real and role play

## The basic idea

Either for real or in role, students conduct interviews to find out what people or characters think, know or feel about any given situation. They use the information gained to produce news reports, interview feature articles, drama scripts, or language investigations.

### Applying it

• Have students role-playing characters conducting interviews of other characters in a text as in Teachit's **Key Stage 4>Prose>Of Mice and Men by John Steinbeck>What happened at Weed**.

• Have students role-playing reporters investigating real life scenarios or a topical issue for a news feature. Teachit resource **Key Stage 3>Media & Non-Fiction>Newspapers> Conduct your own interviews** provides a useful format for this.

• Have students interviewing each other about their language biographies, or people they know with interesting personal language stories to tell, and writing feature articles. Students could adapt Teachit's **Language Library>Language Acquisition> Personal language histories** as their starting point.

### What's the point?

Good interviewing requires a challenging mixture of empathy with the subject and a clarity and sharpness that enables them to push (sensitively) past any obfuscation. That takes practice but also a bit of nouse which doesn't always get valued in education, so that makes it worth doing for a start. Some unexpected students shine in interviewing, especially when the interviews are real. As a creative practice for literary study, it tends to produce more subtle character analysis.

### Tricks of the trade

Make the interview have a point. This means ensuring that the information gained will be used in some subsequent task. It's also worth spending time with students working on good interview technique, looking at issues such as how you make your subject comfortable (or deliberately uncomfortable), the difference between types of questions, how you get to the truth etc. Encourage students to experiment.

### Variations on a theme

• I like to start the academic year off with a new group with an opportunity for them to conduct a class interview of me. Yeah, they ask you all the stuff about marital status (and the rest...), but just reserve the right before you start not to answer any personal questions and they will soon be onto useful things like classroom ground rules and what kinds of beatings you give.

### Whizzing it

Get the digital recording equipment out (audio or video or student mobile phones with a speech recording function) and have students producing their own vox pops on any subject you like. Instead of standard essays on environmental issues, or gun running, or whatever is topical, get them producing webpages for *Newsround* with young people's voices a prominent feature.

# In the manner of

Experimenting with different ways of saying and doing

## The basic idea

Students experiment with a different manner of saying things: a word, a phrase, a line. Or with different ways of behaving or performing a role. Think adverbs.

### Applying it

- To develop an understanding of adverbs (well, adverbs of manner, anyway) get students out on the back field on a sunny afternoon for some walking around. Shout out an adverb: they have to walk in that manner. Easy.

- Experiment with different ways of reading some lines or sections of a poem. Students pull an adverb card out of a bag and try it out. They keep changing the card until they find something that works really well. Present and discuss alternatives and their consequences for meaning and interpretation.

- Students perform a scene in the manner of. Give different groups different adverbs to work with. When they present their performance the rest of the class has to guess the adverb. Discuss alternatives and their consequences. See a well worked example in Teachit's *Key Stage 3>Drama>Twelfth Night> Interpreting characters and action in Twelfth Night - Act 2 Scene 5*.

### What's the point?

In its simplest form, bodily intelligence is used to help students remember the concept of the adverbial of manner. Different learning styles just mix it up a bit, especially on a sunny day. In the performance applications, its point is smarter, encouraging creative experimentation with meaning and interpretation, and helping to break down the idea of the text as holy relic.

### Tricks of the trade

As with all performance work, warn your classroom neighbours, or invest your birthday money in soundproofing, or sleep with the drama teacher for a classroom swap. After that, it's a question of making sure students have interesting adverbs to work with, and a range of possibilities to try out. Don't just give them one that they have to do at all costs – testing to destruction and then tinkering around with five other ideas is healthy creative practice not an annoying waste of time.

### Variations on a theme

- For a quieter activity, try rewriting passages or scenes in a different manner, eg the eyeball gouging scene of *King Lear* comically (might as well, as every class I've ever taught it to always laughs anyway...). Draws out writer's choices and their consequences.

- Have an 'extra' person in each performance group whose job it is to take digital photos so that interpretations can be explored more fully later.

- Reflections on which of the 'in the manner of' performance experiments worked best and why would be a productive use of time.

### Whizzing it

Get the photos off the camera and onto the PC for multimedia presentations of work rather than repeat performances.

# Jackets

Create them/explore literary interpretations

## The basic idea

Develop interpretations of texts. Either design and create new book jackets in as much detail as you like: images, font-happiness, author profiles, blurbs and puffs. Or explore the interpretations offered by different existing alternatives: either raid your book cupboard or look at the images of editions available on Amazon (try UK and US for more variations).

### Applying it

- Works a treat with the heavy hitting classics as the dozens of different editions highlight a wide variety of different interpretations. Try Jane Austen's *Pride and Prejudice*, Charlotte Bronte's *Jane Eyre*, Charles Dickens' *Great Expectations*, Robert Louis Stevenson's *Treasure Island*…

- Not as many but really interesting variations in the jackets of modern classics such as John Steinbeck's *Of Mice and Men*, Harper Lee's *To Kill A Mockingbird*, George Orwell's *1984*, and F. Scott Fitzgerald's *The Great Gatsby*.

- Do *A Midsummer Night's Dream* and decide how many fairies it really takes to make a decent book jacket. Challenge students not to include any.

- Check out **http://www.ziv.jerusalem.k12.il/eng jacket.doc** for a useful DIY template.

### What's the point?

Both activities support much discussion and debate about interpretations of the text. These can be discussed in isolation, but it can also be highly motivating for students with an applied or entrepreneurial orientation to connect it all up to real world issues of publishing. What's interesting? What sells?

In the DIY variation the brevity of the form encourages precise selection of comments and quotations, and lively pithy description. In the existing versions activity, get students choosing their favourite and justifying it. Scope in the process for lots of comparative analysis, critical evaluation, heated debate and verbal horse-trading.

### Tricks of the trade

Popular, classic, pre-twentieth century texts often work best for the exploration of existing jackets, as there can be almost as many options as there are students in your class. To encourage more thoughtful evaluation, start off by giving each student one jacket. Get them to think carefully about what it shows, maybe jot down a few notes, and then hurl everything into the group discussion mix. Alternatively, help to develop the quality of the group discussion of each jacket by using **Opinion cards** (see page 94).

### Variations on a theme

- Works really well as a pre-reading task. Students are invited to look at a range of book jacket images and decide from this information what it is about. Themes, characters, setting, mood. Explore expectations of storyline and style.

- Also works well at Advanced Level in exploring alternative critical perspectives. Which images go with which kind of theoretical interpretation?

- Give some students the specific challenge of creating a jacket that represents a particular critical perspective.

- As a post-reading activity the critical question is, 'Which jacket best sums up your overall interpretation of the text?'

- Find a local publisher to give a talk and/or judge covers.

### Whizzing it

Set a template up on your school/college network and let students play around with it to their heart's content. Set the template up so that it's the right size for their copy of the text, get them printing off their versions in glorious technicolour and then teach them the long-lost art of book-covering. Have a template with the right spine width and folding space at the edges. Task a student with the design task? Find a technology teacher who will trade you a template for a new sliding bevel?

# Jigsaw discussion

Discussion technique for maximum participation

## The basic idea

Okay, pay attention because this can seem complicated until you get your head round it. Start by forming groups for discussion, let's say fours. Give each group the same text or task to work on. They do some preliminary general investigation. Then you move to the second round. In this you set as many specific focuses for further investigation as there are students. Each student in the group takes responsibility for one of these according to their interest. You form new specialist focus groups consisting of all the students working on that issue. They work on it together. Then you move to the third round. The original base groups are reformed. Each student reports back on their specialist group's findings. Then they see what overarching conclusions they can draw from this work.

### Applying it

• Take a scene from a play or a section of a novel with multiple characters in it. Assign one character to each student for the specialist focus groups. For an example of this see Teachit's **Key Stage 3>Prose> Gulliver's Travels>A range of well designed worksheets**. To extend the challenge, set concluding round questions that invite comparison of characters.

• Works well with any text for preparation for essay writing, with students looking separately at themes, language, structure, and then pooling their ideas. Teachit's **Key Stage 4> Prose>Of Mice and Men by John Steinbeck>Animal imagery in the novel** could easily be used as a jigsaw discussion.

• Try it with poetry at any key stage, either by giving students a set of poems to divide out between them for closer investigation, or each student taking responsibility for a stanza for microscopic analysis.

### What's the point?

Every student in the class has to take responsibility for the learning that happens. They say there is nothing so powerful for learning as teaching, and in this activity students have to teach each other what they have learned in their specialist group. It encourages a collaborative approach, requires students to work with other students in the class without removing them completely from their friendship groups, and involves a lot of discussion and student responsibility for discussion. It also breaks up extended discussion physically into different rounds, which can help to prevent thinking getting sluggish.

### Tricks of the trade

Concentrate on careful instruction giving at each stage as it can be a bit confusing for students when they first encounter this technique. Watch carefully at the transition stages to make sure everyone ends up where they should be. In preparation, make sure there are separate and meaningful tasks at each stage, which go beyond just the pooling of information and into transforming, applying or extending it in some way.

### Variations on a theme

• To speed it up, set specialist focus tasks that can be answered without additional resources and from existing student knowledge, and make the final phase about developing a straightforward set of notes or giving an informal presentation to the class.

• To slow it down, set tasks that require research and investigation in the library or using the internet, and make the final activity a formal presentation or a richer and more demanding written task. Several lessons can be spent in highly productive activity with almost no input from you if you set it up well.

# Jigsaw puzzles
Find the pieces, put them together

## The basic idea

Take a series of large pictures and cut each one up into four or five pieces. Reproduce on card and laminate for multiple re-use where possible. Shuffle the pieces up and give each student one. Then they have to get up, move about, piece together their puzzle. Then they sit in that group and do whatever it is you want them to do next.

### Applying it

• Make each puzzle an interesting photograph or painting. Once the jigsaw puzzle has been completed, the group collaborates to develop ideas for a story.

• Create the puzzles from different stills of the film version of your text. Once students are together, their job is to work on that scene or moment in some way.

• Want something more challenging? Make each puzzle the stanzas from a poem. Needs a lot of debate to sort the pieces out, so works best in a smaller class.

### What's the point?

First of all it gets students up and moving, and that can mix up the dynamic very constructively for students who have lots of physical energy in class. It seems to cause irreparable psychological damage to anyone over the age of sixteen - 'Awwwwwww, why do we have to mooooooove?'- but that just makes it even more good for them, and satisfies your evil teacher streak if they've been getting on your nerves lately. The underlying point to this is to move students out of their comfort zone by getting them to work with different students in the class. This can challenge them to think much more sharply, and to interact socially with others, and to value each other's strengths by coming to know them better. The completion of the puzzle requires useful levels of collaboration and discussion.

### Tricks of the trade

Have nice big puzzle pieces so they can see what they've each got. Start it off assertively by making them all stand up and move into some kind of a space. If you don't do this, the danger is they will yawn and lean backwards and just start passing the pieces around. Have a rule if you need it that the puzzle piece is not allowed to leave their hand until they place it in the puzzle. Expect a high level of noise once they get started. This is integral to the activity so either let them get on with it and smile sweetly at the person glaring through the classroom door, or challenge the students to do it in silence through mime and gesture. I'm all for noise, myself…

### Variations on a theme

• Set it up as a race if you're short of time or need to up the ante a bit generally, with an enormous gift (honour? glory?) to the winning team.

• Use it as a way into exploring effective communication by having observers note one student's performance in the activity. Use to draw out ideas about what helped this collaborative task and what didn't.

### Whizzing it

The whole point is physical movement so not much use there but you might have the completed images available on the network for use in follow up work.

# Journals

Reading logs, learning logs and blogs

## The basic idea

Get students recording what happens day by day, week by week, in the time honoured tradition of journal keeping. Individual or collective. Nice little book with a padlock on the front, or make ultra-funky bloggers of 'em all: same thing.

### Applying it

• The timeless old chestnut: get students keeping a reading log, recording all the books they read, their thoughts, reflections, star ratings, whatever…

• Another variation of the reading log is for students to record their thoughts, reflections, feelings, whatever, as they read through a set text. Don't set questions or notes: let them respond personally, creatively, honestly, emotively. Encourage creativity and depth of response.

• Get students keeping a learning log in the subject, which brings together their learning in the classroom and outside, e.g. things they've read, or seen on the telly, or looked up on the internet, conversations they've had, poems they've written.

### What's the point?

It encourages students to keep track of their learning – seeing it build up in a tangible way can be very motivating for some students. If set up in the right way, it brings together classroom learning and the far wider world our students actually live in, and it values connections they make between those worlds. Again, very motivating for some students to be 'allowed' to talk about their passion for Terry Pratchett novels, or something about language that they observed in action. It can provide a very fruitful basis for discussion about their progress and give you a real insight into individual interests that you can draw on to plan teaching, or to help students set more individual goals.

For students who feel a bit alienated or steamrollered by the whole formal curriculum thing, the fact that they have ownership of its content makes it probably the most important thing they will do. And it gets students writing without any need whatsoever for us to mark it – indeed the magic spell is broken if you do anything other than invite students to talk about what they have written…

*(continued over)*

### Tricks of the trade

You can't set journal keeping and a whole ton of homework so if you want it to happen you have to make space for it, either within a reasonable homework frame, or within the classroom. Be assertive about it when you start, checking it, bigging it up, getting students to share things frequently – until they get into a regular habit. It's actually much easier to monitor if you set it up as a blog – see whizzy section below. A good trick is to give students the choice of how many entries they make per week – between one and three, say – and how much you expect – from one to three paragraphs, for example. That gives them flexibility if they get loads of Maths homework one week, or a bad headache, and sends the message that you trust them to make a sensible decision. Then they'll probably all write loads…

### Variations on a theme

• Go to town on creativity by giving them a scrapbook to fill as a kind of visual log instead of making them do loads of writing. They can stick articles in, pictures of the covers of novels they've read, photos of things they've done related to the subject (e.g. class or family trips), etc. Insist on some annotation. This worked brilliantly as a summer log project for students moving into A2 English Language: their task was to produce a log for eight weeks of all the things they came across about language that interested them. Not allowed to start A2 unless the scrapbook was full and appropriately annotated.

### Whizzing it

First teach students about appropriate measures for staying safe on the internet. Then go to **www.blogger.com** or equivalent and get them all signed up with their own blog (free, takes 3 minutes, idiotproof). For safety, especially if they are under 16, make sure they use a cyber-name and don't give their email address, any other contact details, or personal information out. For tighter security, you might prefer to do this on your school/college learning platform (e.g. Blackboard or WebCT).

Then they blog merrily away, keeping their reading log or learning log online. They can upload pictures, text, audio files, whatever they like, in their very own corner of webspace. You could then save all the URLs in a folder in your favourites. Alternatively, set up a class blog. In this format, everyone can contribute and you've only got to look in one place, though possibly more difficult if you have a large class to keep track of who's contributing. You could get students taking turns to update what has been learned after each lesson, with others chipping in with extra comments, bits missed etc…

# Jumbled texts

Mix it up then sort it out

## The basic idea

Take two texts, any two similar texts that you want to work on, and chop them into chunks – lines, stanzas, paragraphs, as you like. Or if your class has been really mean and you need to show who's boss, take multiple texts. Students have to create order out of the chaos of pieces, recreating the original text(s) in the correct sequence.

### Applying it

• Start comparisons of poems off with jumbled texts. Try it with Heather Buck's poem 'Evening' and T.S. Eliot's 'Preludes'. Or William Blake's 'Tyger' and Laurie Lee's 'Town Owl'. Or two of Blake's poems, one from *Songs of Innocence* and its parallel poem from *Songs of Experience*.

• Take a tabloid and a compact broadsheet article on the same story and jumble them up. Now how much difference can we say there is between the two?

• Compare character descriptions. Try jumbling the portraits of the Wife of Bath and the Prioress from the *General Prologue to the Canterbury Tales*, or the Monk and the Priest, or any pair you or your students think make for interesting comparison.

### What's the point?

It takes very close reading to complete this activity, paying attention to details of language and style as well as form and content. This makes it a good lead-in to full discussion of these features, as well as comparative analysis where appropriate. Puzzles are very satisfying for many students, and it comes as a welcome relief for some that just occasionally there is such a thing as a right answer in an English lesson.

### Tricks of the trade

Choose good texts and try them out on a friend first! If they are too similar the task will get frustrating, a good thing at a certain pitch but watch carefully for the pain/boredom threshold. If they are too obvious the activity will be a pointless waste of space and your students will quite rightly tell you so.

### Variations on a theme

• To mix it up, try giving different students different sized chunks. Individual lines or sentences make it very challenging, whole stanzas or paragraphs are easier. You can decide this in advance, or let them choose the level of challenge they feel up to. Don't assume it'll be your A* students who are best at this; they may well be, but some other students will be natural born puzzlers and they should get a chance to sharpen their teeth on something harder too.

• See **Intercutting** (page 59) for a creative application of this activity.

### Whizzing it

Put each of the chopped up sections into a text box in Word and you have a ready-made activity for use on the interactive whiteboard. Useful for working through the answers collectively.

# Juxtapositions

Comparisons without the jumbling...

## The basic idea

An entirely straightforward no bells and whistles technique, involving the simple juxtaposition of two or more things, in order that one illuminates the other by comparison. Invite straightforward comparative discussion, provide light scaffolding with some questions, or hefty scaffolding with a grid: all good.

### Applying it

• Juxtapose two film versions of the text, or clips of key scenes from two or more. A classic classroom activity. See Teachit's *Key Stage 3/4> Drama>Romeo and Juliet> Compare two film versions of Romeo and Juliet*. Or *Media Library>Frankenstein films> Compare 1931 version of Frankenstein to the 1997 Branagh version*. Check out the different versions of *A Midsummer Night's Dream*, or any text, on the Internet Movie Database at **www.imdb.com**.

• Juxtapose pages from the novel and its dramatic adaptation (or vice versa). For oven-ready resources like this on *His Dark Materials* and *Rabbit-Proof Fence*, check out the *NATE Drama Packs*. Also available in single book form is E. Annie Proulx's short story and the *Brokeback Mountain* screenplay.

• Juxtapose different forms with a thematic or stylistic connection as in Teachit's resource comparing how two writers make incredible events credible in *Key Stage 4>Genre>Comparing texts>The Withered Arm and Mrs Midas*.

• For higher level work, try comparing source material and text as in Teachit's resource comparing Plutarch's account of *Coriolanus* with Shakespeare's treatment *Key Stage 5>Drama>Coriolanus>From Plutarch to Shakespeare*.

### What's the point?

Comparison and contrast are essential thinking skills, and tasks which invite this in increasingly challenging ways will develop increasingly sophisticated skills. The more unexpected or unusual the juxtaposition, the richer the discussion is likely to be, but this also helps to develop a more flexible and creative mind-set as students are edged out of their comfort zone and into really productive learning.

### Tricks of the trade

Try to make sure there is a real point to the comparison rather than just as a hamster-wheel activity otherwise some students will lose interest within three and a half minutes. This really means connecting the knowledge that is gained from the activity to some higher purpose: expressive writing, or an essay, or production of a genre 'recipe', or a timeline showing variation patterns, or whatever can be dreamed up to make creative use of the learning.

### Variations on a theme

• Instead of deepening the well worn grooves of the same old comparisons, mix it up a bit. Get students bringing in their own texts from popular culture to juxtapose with the set text: films, manga comics, songs, photo stories, whatever rocks their boat. It will serve the same purpose of illuminating the set text but with a zillion times more engagement. Try it with poems in the GCSE anthology.

• Two poems or short stories is fine as a juxtaposition for many students, but stretch the stronger ones with bigger tasks, like several novels. They can handle it... Another option is to play a game of chicken with your class. Start them off with two texts. When that juxtaposition is well underway, offer anyone who thinks they can handle it another text. It won't necessarily be your boffs who go for this – they may be quite happy dissecting every fibre of two. And another. And another. Instead of predicting what they might be able to handle, challenge them! This encourages them to test their limits, which some students find exciting and to take intellectual risks. So what if they 'fail'? They will learn 36 times as much by doing so. As long as you debrief and evaluate sensitively.

# Kangaroo Court

Conducting a mock trial

## The basic idea

Take a baddie in your book and put him/her on trial. Some students are counsel for the defence, some counsel for the prosecution. Throw in a judge, a jury and assorted witnesses and you've got a great lesson in store.

### Applying it

- For a detailed resource with all the role cards and instructions you need, check out Teachit's resource for conducting the trial of Mrs Kay and Mr Briggs in **Key Stage 3/4>Drama> Our Day Out by Willy Russell> Speaking and Listening task**.

- Explore the culpability of the Nurse and Friar Laurence in *Romeo and Juliet*. More excellent all-you-can-eat resources in Teachit's **Key Stage 4> Drama>Romeo and Juliet: Romeo and Juliet: The Trial**. In my classroom Macbeth has been tried countless times for high treason and a string of murders – he even got off once...

- Adapt the resources above for any characters in any text. Lord Asriel and/or Mrs Coulthard from *His Dark Materials*. Professor Snape from *Harry Potter*. Heathcliff from *Wuthering Heights* for cruelty to children and animals, false imprisonment and mental torture.

### What's the point?

Students generally get right into this because they've seen so much court-room action on TV. It's great for stimulating debate, with students on both sides of the bench having to really think about the best evidence to use to support their case, and the jury having to weigh that carefully. It includes a good variety of roles, so everyone can participate in a way that plays to their strengths and interests, making it a lovely activity to get a bit of whole class bonding going. It's also an effective way of drawing out ideas about the students' interpretation of the text, particularly where serious moral questions are explored. It has clear links to the development of citizenship and the oral skills of effective argument.

### Tricks of the trade

Select your judge carefully: you need someone with the charisma and authority to preside effectively over the courtroom to make sure it doesn't descend into chaos. You might like to play this role! To help with this, make sure everyone has a clear idea about how the case will proceed: there is a fantastic free guide for teachers at **www.citizenshipfoundation.org.uk**. You also need to make sure you debrief the students afterwards, getting everyone to come back into their normal role as a student in your classroom. Simple debrief questions could include 'How did you feel when you were in role?' and 'What did you learn from this activity?' It's important to capture and reflect on the learning that takes place or it can easily get lost in all the fun. It is possible to do this in one reasonably sized lesson if the students are already very familiar with the text. Otherwise, it is better to have at least one lesson to prepare it and one to do the trial in.

### Variations on a theme

- This activity provides for easy differentiation by interest, or readiness or learning profile as there are so many different ways of adapting the roles. Students who prefer to listen might make good jurors; involve the verbally argumentative in the defence/prosecution counsel teams and watch them shine; get those who like making imaginative responses to situations in the text to be witnesses.

- If you haven't got time/inclination/ sufficient crowd control measures for the full monty, find a character guilty of some trumped up charges and then get the class debating the sentence. Great for teasing out their interpretations of events. See an example in Teachit's **Key Stage 3>Drama>Collision Course by Nigel Hinton>The trial of Raymond Whitfield**.

### Whizzing it

If you have enough time, video the trial and get some students to edit it for future use in class and/or reflection on the learning that took place.

# Killjoys

A focus on exam preparation techniques

## The basic idea

Revision is the most boring activity known to humanity, after which the exams are a lively relief. Its general effect is to create high levels of anxiety amongst students and teachers, bring out the most ineffective teaching and learning, and encourage dependence. Precisely the opposite, then, of what we vaguely intend. But, needs must when the devil drives, so here are some more productive techniques.

## Applying it

- Don't give them sample A* answers to pore/weep over; give them C/D grade answers and get them to rewrite them. Best if you have the text in electronic format so they can cut and paste, insert, delete and generally muck about with the original. Or set this task with answers a grade below each student's personal goal.

- Get students to write their own exam paper. Give them a past paper to model exactly but don't give them a template: the act of typing out the rubric might help them absorb the instructions. Then they choose questions, texts, etc.

- When they've done that, give them a mark scheme from an old paper and get them to model that too for their own questions. That's a more challenging task but a very worthwhile one.

- For GCSE, practise rapid accurate selection of anthology texts to go with any kind of question. Put enlarged text titles on big cards. Put enlarged thematic or stylistic issues they could get asked a question about on big cards. Draw a question and stick it on the board. Groups race to choose three poems they could write about and stick them under the question card. If the rest of the class agree that their selection is sound they win a point; if not, award bonus points for the next group's try, etc...

## hat's the point?

All of these approaches are focused on the exam but they allow a bit more scope for students to play around with the materials of the exam rather than fixating on them as some kind of dangerous beast. That will encourage more relaxed and more creative thinking, a far more useful commodity than exam hall brain-freeze.

## Tricks of the trade

It's boring, so try and make it fun. It's a solitary pursuit that ruthlessly exposes all one's individual shortcomings so try to make lessons about shared experience and collaboration. It's about what they can now do, having followed a principled and well taught course of study - so stop feeding the frenzy.

## Variations on a theme

- Encourage academic blag and bluster as exam skills that can be useful in making a little learning go a long way. Play competitive blagging about texts and poems, using Radio 4's *Just a Minute* programme format with bonus prizes for accurate use of academic phrasing and appropriate terminology. Make the other students judge it.

# Kim's game

That lovely QUIET parlour game...

## The basic idea

Adapted version of the old parlour game, in which a set of items is placed in a bag or on a tray or table. It's best if students can pick the items up, turn them around, have a good look. They get a specified amount of time in which to memorise all the items. Then the items are put back in the bag or covered up and students have to remember what they saw. Extravagant prizes for achieving a new personal best and/or breaking the class record.

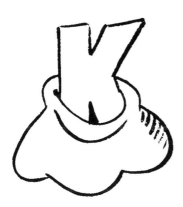

### Applying it

• 15 key words that need spelling accurately or terms to be remembered. Or short quotations for a closed book exam text, written on memory-aid objects or illustrated cards. Or written on chocolate bars (or on tags on mini-chocs!) – they get to keep every perfectly accurate item of recall...

• As a pre-reading exercise to generate interest, put ten things in the bag that Defoe's Robinson Crusoe used from the shipwreck to help him survive, or ten objects from the island in Golding's *Lord of the Flies*. Play the game, individually or in groups, then devise shipwreck stories with as many items as each person/pair/team remembers. Then lead into the reading, noting what each of the ten items is used for as it appears in the novel.

### What's the point?

Simple: it can help to develop memory which is obviously a very useful tool for certain types of learning. It also encourages concentration. Use it to develop discussion of different ways of memorising objects or information, and link this to exploration of students' preferred learning styles.

### Tricks of the trade

Pick a quirky variety of objects to stimulate speculation, interest, and ways of the information sticking in the students' minds. The other key trick is to think about how much silent recall your students will manage. Whilst it would be nice to have 35 minutes of uninterrupted daydreaming while they attempt to remember 176 items, that only happens in the Fantasy League School. The shorter the attention span the fewer the items to be memorised. Don't be worried if that's lower than you'd like: aim to build up both concentration span and recall accuracy over time.

### Variations on a theme

• Get the students making up the object bags themselves as selecting items to represent the information will aid the memory process. Give different groups of students different bags according to the level of challenge or interest required.

• Work over a period of time to increase memory, by getting them to draw a bar chart on a piece of file paper. Number of items memorised (keep it the same each time) goes up the side, date of game goes along the bottom. Each time they colour in their score. The challenge is either to improve or hold steady at a high level.

### Whizzing it

Get groups of students to prepare a Kim's game PowerPoint on a given topic with one revision 'object' on each slide. Animated at a certain speed like the *Generation Game* conveyor belt. Save these up and use as quick-fire revision.

# King or Queen of the classroom
Spelling intimidation fun

## The basic idea

Have the students lined up round the classroom. The person at the front of the line steps into the question zone. They get asked a question. If they get the answer right, they stay there and take another question. If they get it wrong they join the end of the line and the next student steps into the zone. Give everyone some lives so they stay in the game longer, but the point is to keep going until only one person is left in and they become king or queen of the classroom.

### Applying it

• Fun thing to do as your Christmas special, with general knowledge questions, questions about literature, or complete trivia.

• Do it as a spelling bee if you've got a class that can handle that. Worked brilliantly with my A Level class to make the point that their general standard of spelling was atrocious. And they thought I was letting them play a game…

• Useful for livening revision up a bit – have any kind of questions you like about the text or topic.

### What's the point?

It puts students on the spot and under pressure to recall knowledge they should have. This gets them used to handling exam pressure, and can build confidence to trust their intellectual instincts. Because it's rapid fire and

students are standing up, it changes the classroom dynamic and that can be a useful thing, keeping them on their toes literally and figuratively, and bringing an unexpected dimension into the classroom. It's nothing fancy but a change is very often as good as a rest.

### Tricks of the trade

Keep the questions coming at a rapid fire pace. This game is adapted from a tennis training drill and it's good to think of it like that – get one person out of the hitting zone and the next person into it without breaking your questioning rhythm. The point is fast and furious – if it becomes lackadaisical you start getting into classroom management issues. As people lose all their lives and have to sit out, try to keep them involved. Have them joining a similarly rotating line to step up and fire the questions, as this will keep their brains ticking – and most students enjoy the power! One other thing: make sure you've got enough questions to play! Do the maths…

### Variations on a theme

• Instead of you setting the questions, get the students all contributing some. To avoid overlap, allocate specific things for them to prepare questions on. Appoint a questioner from the students and join in! This can really add a bit of 'edge' to the situation, with students competing much more fiercely just to make sure you don't win. Especially if there's a prize!

• Play doubles instead of singles, with pairs stepping up to answer the questions. Nice if you have pressure-sensitive students you need to build up a bit.

### Whizzing it

If you want to go hi-tech, you could have the questions flashing up on the big screen in an animated powerpoint. If the students aren't quick enough the question will disappear before they've had a chance to answer it. That'll keep 'em moving.

# Kiss of life

Or how experienced teachers manage to roll with the punches

## The basic idea

Teaching is a combat sport. You're lying on the floor winded by the pace and intensity of it all. Not much choice but to keep going till the end of term. You've got a lesson tomorrow that you just can't get your head round. All you want to do is crawl into bed. What do you do? Easy answer. From your teacher's emergency survival box you pull out a **Kiss of Life** lesson – something single-lesson and stand-alone, with no marking, that involves minimal teacher input, and keeps the students busy, quiet and occupied. Don't sweat the small stuff, concentrate on the bonus to the school/students of you being there at all...

### Applying it

- Over time, write a 'spare' lesson for each scheme of work that meets these criteria. 20-30-40-50 things they need to find out about the writer or text. An online self-marking multiple choice quiz. An extra video or DVD.

- Get them browsing the online OED and using the schools materials available there for dictionary work: hours of stuff there. Or finding a number of interesting texts to use next lesson (by which time you will have planned it...) from 'Texts in Context' at **www.bllearning.co.uk/live/text/** .

- Use Teachit oven-ready online lesson packs, such as *Whizzy things> Online lessons>Introduction to Shakespeare*. The first lesson is a nice tidy little webquest that could easily take a whole lesson of mild-mannered browsing, the *As You Like It* lesson could stand alone very nicely. All you need is a PC suite and a Teachit subscription.

- Give students 20 websites about the topic or text or writer to explore, evaluate and write reviews of. Then they've got their own revision resources guide.

### What's the point?

Survival. A bit of learning. Sometimes that's enough.

### Tricks of the trade

Don't let on to your students that you're doing this. Telling them you're too exhausted to think and you're going to take the foot off the accelerator for a lesson is as good as asking them all to throw off their ties, put their feet on the desks and get into an exuberant holiday spirit that will only give you a bigger headache than you started the lesson with. The lines are: 'You've all been working so hard that I thought we'd have a slight change of focus today,' or 'We'll come back to that next lesson, but I've been noticing we need to spend a bit more time on xyz.'

### Variations on a theme

- See **Writing kick starts** (page 146) for more specific ideas about narrative work. These require a bit more effort than your full fat **Kiss of life** lesson, but can be useful nonetheless.

- At the start of each term tell the students they are going to have the opportunity for five minutes of fame and glory talking to the rest of the class about their favourite interest, life experience, hobby, whatever, and that they should prepare themselves to be able to do this at any time. Not an assessed speaking and listening assignment – just five minutes of talk. Save it up for when you need a breather.

# Labelling
Variation on the cloze theme

## The basic idea

Take or create an image or a diagram. Stick labels on it. Simple, huh? You can go ultra-simple with plain old annotation but there is something about sticking labels on that is deeply satisfying… Too much time spent with sticker books as a child, maybe?...

### Applying it

- Label a diagram of the Globe theatre following research about it as in Teachit's *Key Stage 3>Drama> Introduction to Shakespeare: background and biography> Research the Globe theatre*.

- Use labels to annotate a text. Teachit's resource *Key Stage 3/4> Much Ado About Nothing – Act 3>Annotate the scene* has all the labels that go to produce an annotated version of the text 'dropped on the floor'. Students have to pick them up and put them in the right place before writing a set of director's notes.

- Create and label a picture of a character with key characterisation quotations. For a simple version see Teachit's *Key Stage 4>Prose>Of Mice and Men by John Steinbeck> Chapter 4 - Getting to know Crooks*. Easily adapted for any text and key stage.

- For revision of the GCSE anthology get them labelling the poems in the style of 'Friends' episodes: 'The one with…'

- Get labelling film stills from the adaptation of your text with captions, speech bubbles with pertinent quotation, or analytical comments.

### What's the point?

It's nothing fancy, but it can help to develop concise thinking due to the pithy nature of labels. Because it demands a small level of physical engagement with the text, it seems to encourage a greater sense of commitment to it. Using sticky labels may seem a bit daft, but it often has the curious effect of encouraging more discussion and debate, as students know that once it's on they're committed to it. Especially if you refuse to give them any replacement stickers or clean texts…

### Tricks of the trade

There's not much that can go wrong with this, it's so simple, but make sure the task is worth doing because new learning will take place, and that it's part of some richer overall design.

### Variations on a theme

- Turn it on its head and give students a diagram that has been incorrectly or poorly labelled; get them to sort it out.

- This works well as a five-minute starter activity. Before studying a scene, put a still from it up on the big screen and have pairs buzzing ideas for labels.

### Whizzing it

Labelling activities work well on the big screen or PCs. Arrows, speech bubbles, text boxes – clicker-happy students will be in heaven.

# Lectures

Because A Level students sure do need the practice

## The basic idea

The teacher stands at the front and delivers a long verbal presentation on a topic, usually from about 40 minutes to an hour in length. This may or may not be supported by visual cues or handouts. Most teachers avoid this kind of presentation like the plague, certainly in Key Stages three and four, but by the time you get to Key Stage five it starts sneaking in. This may either be deliberate, as an occasional practice to help students to prepare for higher education, or out of fearful belief that they will all fail unless you dictate notes to them, and that somehow students will be able to handle this because they are a few months older. That's unlikely, so if you're going to do it, do it mindfully, with the same attention to checking learning as with the use of any other technique.

### Applying it

- Can be on any text or topic you like, but if I'm doing it with my own class I like to try and position myself in some kind of a guest speaker role, to change the dynamic and make it a bit more formal. So, with Literature A2 students, I've given them a special lecture with more sophisticated ideas about the language of the set text. With A2 Language students, a special lecture on the development of literary language to complement and inform the study of language change.

### What's the point?

Being able to listen thoughtfully for extended periods of time is an important skill for life, so even though some students find it very difficult (me included) and though some will not be planning to go on to higher education, it is well worth doing. By including activities to increase their staying power you can teach them, overtly or implicitly, some techniques for dealing with it positively, especially if auditory forms of learning are very low down on their list of preferences.

### Tricks of the trade

- Think about how you start. As with any kind of lesson, you need a hook that will capture their attention from wherever it's just been. An anecdote, an interesting quotation, a striking visual – all the usual suspects. For bigger hooks, or as follow up to a mini hook, give students all the quotations or examples you are going to use in your lecture and get them brainstorming ideas about how they might fit together in an argument about the text or topic.

- Vary the form of the presentation so that it's not just your essay read out loud, and there is scope for students to interact with the material and bring their own ideas and understanding to it. You could include a problem that needs solving and give students a few minutes to 'buzz' or scribble down their ideas before you carry on.

- Don't put all the points on PowerPoint slides and just read them out – very dull. If you are going to use PowerPoint, get them engaging in note-making more actively. Put the points on the slides but not the examples, so they have to note these, or vice versa. Or make each slide a tabloid style headline that they will have to transform from your input into serious notes. Or make each slide an image that they have to transform into words from your input – or vice versa…

- Think about having spot questions or challenges at various points to keep them on their toes.

- Use the planted questions technique described in **Zombie killers** (page 150) to incorporate pain-free but productive question and answer into the lecture.

- Make sure students have the opportunity to review and discuss the material presented, and to apply it for themselves. Remember Confucius: I hear and I forget. I see and I remember. I do and I understand.

### Variations on a theme

- Take opportunities that arise to have guest lecturers coming into your classroom, or to take students to lecture days for A Level students at universities. Choose carefully, and build your students' stamina up first, as four hour-long lectures in a day is enough to kill off the hardiest undergraduate, never mind a first year A Level student…

### Whizzing it

There are some very nice animated PowerPoint presentations in Teachit's resources, either to use directly or as a model. Check out **Key Stage 4>Poetry>Pre 1914 Poetry>On My First Sonne** PowerPoint presentation and, in the same place, **>The Eagle** PowerPoint.

# Letters

Falling in love with stamps and envelopes

## The basic idea

Students write letters to the author of a text, any kind of text, telling them what they think of their work. Or to the editor of a newspaper in response to an article that was published. Or to a friend recommending a particular book or idea or course of action. Or to their future self. Or, like Fergal Keane's wonderful *Letter to Daniel*, to a new sibling or other relative. Or, in fantasy land, from one character to another character in a novel or play. Or the letter that is mentioned in the novel but doesn't actually appear there. Or an exchange of letters between friends or opponents. Endless possibilities.

### Applying it

• Working on war poetry? Use research into the experience, and reading of poems, to write soldier's letters home. See Teachit's **Key Stage 3/4> Poetry>War poetry>A letter home**. Compare with the real thing: the Cecil Slack archive is a collection of real letters to and from home at **www.greatwar.eril.net**. Developed by Andrew Moore, this site has lots of ideas for other classroom activities too.

• Get students writing persuasive letters to national newspapers. Highlight a refugee's plight in Teachit's **Key Stage 3>Prose>Refugee Boy by Benjamin Zephaniah>Write a letter to a national newspaper**. Argue a parent's view on hanging in Teachit's **Key Stage 4>Media & Non-fiction>Let Him Have It!> Assignment:Write Mr Bentley's letter to the Queen**.

• Macbeth's letter to his wife is a well worn English teacher's path but a good one nonetheless. If you're teaching this on a wet Friday afternoon in November, have Lady Macbeth send him an email or a volley of text messages instead.

• Next time your local newspaper runs a story about how rubbish young people are, get them bombarding the editor with letters to persuade him/her to change this worn out, clichéd editorial tack.

### What's the point?

Even in an age where email, text messaging and i-messaging threaten to kill off the form for ever, letter writing is still a fine expressive art and it has to be worth teaching for that point alone. But also… it encourages thoughtful organisation of ideas, close reading of the text in order to formulate an appropriate response, and demands the use of fluent connected prose.

## Tricks of the trade

Some students will be very unfamiliar with the form. They may be intimidated by it in its formal use, and baffled by it as a means of personal expression. So don't assume they know either how to do it (its formal conventions) or its purpose. The former is easy to teach ('Do it like this…'); the latter takes time and should involve reading fine expressive letters. After all, however cool text messaging is, nothing quite beats the excitement of an envelope on your doormat (except when you're an adult and it's just a bill…). Find a way for them to experience that excitement for real and we may yet save the form from extinction. Start giving stamp books as prizes.

## Variations on a theme

- Next time you're doing imaginative writing, set some or all of them the challenge of writing their story in epistolary form. Or get doing it as a comedy drama – like Radio 4's *Ladies of Letters*.

- Invite the author in to answer the questions and comments made in their letters. Don't let his/her death several centuries ago put you off! Get one of your A Level drama students or a local jobbing actor to dress up and pretend. And don't tell your class this is happening – make it a magical surprise!

- Writing a real letter to a real person they really want to say something to. Check out the 'Letter to…' feature in the Family supplement of the Saturday *Guardian* for inspiration and/or a real publication context.

- Either as themselves or in role, pairs of students write letters to each other as opponents in an ongoing debate. The *Guardian* publishes an epistolary dialogue feature just like this between two people with opposing views on a current affairs issue. The letters need to keep going until there is some kind of resolution, if only an agreement to differ.

## Whizzing it

Well, for instant techno-popularity with your class, you could get them working in pairs, in role as characters emailing each other. Try Teachit's *Shadow of the Minotaur* resource which has students working on the emails sent between different characters: **Key Stage 3>Prose>Shadow of the Minotaur by Alan Gibbons> Write an email**. But really, don't whizz. Encourage handwritten letter writing. It's a beautiful thing.

# Listing

Simple but still useful...

## The basic idea

Any text or topic. Get students making a list of useful information or ideas about it. Stark staringly obvious, but there are a few ways of jazzing it up a bit that are worth having up your sleeve on a rainy afternoon in November.

### Applying it

• Completely straightforward listing can develop understanding of the complexity of a character's dilemma. Try Teachit's **Key Stage 3>Drama> Collision Course by Nigel Hinton> What Ray would say to his father**... in which students list things Ray would tell his father if he could after scene 24 of the play.

• List reasons, for or against or both, in argument and persuasion work. In Teachit's **Key Stage 4>Media & Non-Fiction>Let Him Have It!> Preparation for the letter writing task**, students list reasons why Derek Bentley should not have been hanged.

• Create lists of related poems for anthology revision as in Teachit's **Key Stage 4>Poetry>Poems from different cultures>Links between the poems in cluster 2**.

### What's the point?

It encourages students to select relevant information from the whole text and to express it in a concise form. This makes it easier for students to compare their ideas, especially if the list is sequenced or organised in some way.

### Tricks of the trade

It ain't what you do it's the way that you do it, and that's what gets results, as Bananarama once so memorably sang. Very true here. This list really needs to be part of a bigger design if it's to have a sense of purpose. A list of points ahead of a written or spoken assignment for which that information is needed is worth doing. Listing texts that go together to improve speed and selection skills for an anthology based exam is useful. Getting students to produce personalised checklists of things they need to remember in their next piece of written work is useful. Anything where there is a clear sense of purpose and a sense of the importance of selecting the right information, rather than just writing down fairly random thoughts in a line.

### Variations on a theme

• Straightforward listing is a useful and accessible task, but adding a few constraints can make it more challenging for those students who need a bit more bite. Set everyone a target, such as ten items on the list, but insist that strong students produce double that and then select the ten best ideas with reasons.

• Once students have produced a basic list, get them thinking about it more closely. Have them rank the points in order of importance and number them. Have them sort them out into key points and sub points with appropriate use of numbering or lettering systems or layered bullet points to show this. Have them using icons to distinguish between different kinds of items on their lists.

• Get students producing individual lists with a fixed number of items. Pair them up and charge them with the task of producing a combined list with the same number of fixed items. Build up via groups to whole class collective list, by which point the text or topic will be much debated.

### Whizzing it

Manipulating lists, by moving items up and down, adding icons and bullet points, etc, is made for PC or interactive whiteboard work. Also works well with pair or group collaboration as lists can be cut and pasted into each other for editing.

# Literary critics

Adopting different theoretical perspectives at AS/A2

## The basic idea

Introduce students to some of the major positions in literary theory, e.g. feminism, post-colonialism, postmodernism, and psychoanalytical theory. Focus on what aspects of a literary text each theoretical perspective tends to focus on. Then get students writing critical accounts of their set text, or any other text, from one or more of these perspectives. Discuss what happens, which perspectives individuals feel most affinity with, and how this is helpful to our understanding of literary study.

### Applying it

- Works really well with fairy stories. This can be done as a stand-alone, or as a lead-in to applying the understanding gained to readings of their set texts. I did 'Little Red Riding Hood' with a mixed ability AS Literature group, and then we applied ideas to our reading of *Wuthering Heights*.

- *The Turn of the Screw* also presents rich opportunities for this kind of activity, especially as there is an edition of the text which presents four clearly labelled readings (Marxist, psychoanalytical, feminist and reader-response, if my memory serves me correctly) which can be used to extend the activity further.

- Just about any passage from *Sons and Lovers* works well as all the throbbing undercurrents make the issues fairly obvious for mixed ability classrooms, but you can also challenge stronger students to find more subtle perspectives. And reading it aloud to your class without guffawing is challenge enough for any teacher!

### What's the point?

It encourages much sharper thinking about the ways in which different readers interpret the text. This really appeals to some students, as it takes away some of the flaky, touchy-feely, 'let's all emote together' nature of the subject and gives it a secure analytical foundation. That can be a huge relief for everyone, and it makes for interesting discussions about how literature connects on a theoretical basis with other subjects such as Psychology, Sociology, Art. It also has the important function of preparing students for progression to English Literature degrees, almost all of which include literary theory in the first year; without this they will be in for a major shock.

### Tricks of the trade

Obviously this is a task to be tackled when students are ready for it. It's important for AS/A2 Literature, but it might also make a good challenge for strong students at an earlier stage. The *Turn of the Screw* activity described above was used in a successful 'gifted and talented' workshop for 14-19 year olds. The important thing is to keep your descriptions of the theoretical positions very clear. Try using Teachit's **Key Stage 5>Skills>A/AS Essentials>Overview of literary critical theory** and/or, in the same place, **Literary criticism viewpoint cards**. Alternatively, the English and Media Centre's publication *Text, Reader, Critic* is excellent – a photocopiable set of resources for this and several other advanced areas of literary study. Differentiate wisely so that everyone is able to complete the task by choosing who works on which theory – some are much easier to get your head round than others…

### Variations on a theme

- There are lots of ways of building up gradually to this. Select (or make up) key quotations from literary critics with distinct perspectives on a particular text, and get students debating which quotation belongs to which perspective.

- Refresh or review understanding of the positions by getting students to label descriptions of different theoretical perspectives, or put labels on paragraphs from critical accounts.

- Use this approach not just with written critical accounts but also with spoken ones too, from panel discussions of a set text, or documentaries. Professor Robert Winston's documentary about *Frankenstein* made for excellent discussion of the shortcomings of a biographical approach to literary criticism.

# Maps
## Of places and journeys

## The basic idea

Any combination you like of big paper, lots of pens, real maps, pins, ribbons, collage materials and sticky stuff. Students make or illustrate a map to show aspects of setting or plot. Map/plan of an important building or community in the text, a character's figurative and/or metaphorical journeys, a quest through a fantasy world. Can be applied at all kinds of levels and to all kinds of texts: different scales, different map styles.

### Applying it

• Work on maps to help visualise journeys, such as Gulliver's assorted travels, or places. Maps of islands have a knack of drawing out strong ideas about uses of settings: try it with *Robinson Crusoe, Lord of the Flies, The Tempest*.

• Quest novels are great for mapping activities: try *His Dark Materials* in trilogy or dramatic adaptation.

• Get students mapping the journeys and worlds the characters travel between in some of Shakespeare's plays: *A Midsummer Night's Dream, The Winter's Tale, Othello, King Lear*.

• Get more advanced students mapping both physical and spiritual or emotional journeys.

### What's the point?

Giving a setting a visual form can encourage students to read for detail, whilst mapping out a journey helps to develop a focus on key stages of the plot. It's fun and produces lots of valuable discussion. As a teacher you can see immediately how different students are interpreting the text. It can give a very tangible form to complex ideas about how they perceive the relationship between real and fantasy worlds, old worlds and new worlds, literal and metaphorical journeys. And as the concept of the journey or quest is such a universal archetype, it provides a rich foundation for imaginative writing.

### Tricks of the trade

Make sure students have a rich pool of examples of different mapping styles and approaches to draw on. A classroom display would support this well. Students might want to use symbols as in Ordnance Survey maps, image 'blow-ups' as in many contemporary travel guide maps, hand drawn maps as in Tolkien or everyone's idea of a pirate's treasure map, but there are hundreds of creative possibilities – heat sense maps, anyone?! Other than that, you just need to make sure students (and your teeth-sucking head of department) understand the educational point of this activity so it's not just colouring in.

### Variations on a theme

• Use as the basis for creative writing development. Check out the materials on the 'Hero's Journey' produced by London Gifted and Talented and available at **www.londongt.org >Resources>Hero's Journey**. Use the 12 stages of the hero's journey as the basis for mapping out a quest. Then write it, with or without the 'Storymaker' tool available on this site.

• In the quick version, a sketch map will suffice to give the overall shape of a plot; with more time, maps can be presented, compared, differences of interpretation discussed and imaginative responses created.

• Go 3D!

### Whizzing it

Unleash a frenzy of electronic cutting and pasting to create beautiful illustrated maps (though I shall ever be a fan of the soaked in tea, burnt at the edges school of map making myself...)

# Masks

## What lies beneath

## The basic idea

Scissors, glue, a dawn raid on the Art/Technology departments and lots of imagination. Students make character masks. Two masks, or one double-sided one, to show how a character changes, or surface emotion and hidden emotion, or appearance and reality. Then get students using their masks to perform a scene or pair of scenes, from the script or adapted from novel, short story or poem.

### Applying it

• At least one theatre company has had a nationwide tour of *Animal Farm* performed with masks. Great project...

• Lots of fun to be had with *Dr Jekyll and Mr Hyde*: combine with the *Ninety Second Version* and you've got several lessons sorted immediately.

• Iago is an obvious choice for the two faced character, but what about Othello's changing faces? How about double-sided masks to show Macbeth at the start and Macbeth at the end?

### What's the point?

To make the two masks distinct, students have to concentrate sharply on the contrasts in the character's attitude, appearance and behaviour. This demands close reading of different sections of the text, comparative analysis, and creative thinking. When teaching plays, it encourages students to think about dramatic performance and can lead to interesting discussion of how the actor might convey this inner tension without a mask. It may well make your kinaesthetic learners very happy, especially if you can trade staffroom favours for a lesson swap with your art department – trade rooms, trade lessons, team teach a joint project...

### Tricks of the trade

Have nice creative materials that students want to get their hands on, and plenty of ideas about types of masks for students who are not too familiar with the form. Try **www.dltk-kids.com>*Search>Masks*** for a basic eye-shape template either for the creatively challenged, or if you are short of time/resources for anything more freeform. Plan the lesson to allow time for discussion, analysis of relevant sections of the text and development of ideas before you let them loose on the fun stuff. Make sure they understand that they are going to have to justify their creative choices later.

### Variations on a theme

• Many variations are possible. Paper plate masks, simple eye masks, top half of the head, elaborate whole head confections, etc.

• Works well individually and as a group design project. To structure the latter, try giving students roles to play e.g. text adviser, creative producer, presenter. This enables students who aren't keen on creative doings to play a different part in the proceedings.

### Whizzing it

Get students to take close-up digital photos of the masks being worn, or record the masked performances with a digital video camera. These can then be explored in the whole class context using the data projector and screen.

# Matching

The rice and pasta of the English teaching profession

## The basic idea

Ever popular staple with a zillion and three applications. Students are given a pile of information and they have to match the parts that go together. Most commonly it's a case of finding the matching pairs; sometimes matching trios. Lots of formats for this: lining statements up on an interactive whiteboard; playing advanced snap; matching a lettered statement from column A with a numbered statement from column B; but by far and away the most popular is the card sort. Information goes on cards, students move them around to find the pairs. Happy times with a photocopier and a guillotine; throw in a laminator and I'm yours….

## Applying it

- Match words and images. In Teachit's **Key Stage 3/4>Macbeth Act 2>'Is this a dagger' speech** six quotations have to be matched to six simple images. Also try matching news headlines to photographs, and speeches to film or production stills.

- Match themes to quotations. Can be done as a straightforward card sort, or try it dominoes style, as in Teachit's **Key Stage 3/4>Romeo and Juliet>Theme dominoes cut out cards.** Easily adapted for any text.

- If you like matching games, play snap. Teachit has lots of Flash snap games for use on the IWB. Put 'snap' in the search box and check out **To Kill A Mockingbird snap, Personal Pronoun snap** and several *Much Ado About Nothing* snaps.

- For a focus on language, match words to etymological origins as in Teachit's **Language library>Language change>Language triplets**. This goes beyond pairs and into trio matching. Also in trios, match key words from a text to their synonyms and antonyms as in **Key Stage 3>Prose>Introducing Mr Dickens>Word Chart 1**.

## What's the point?

The task requires careful reading to identify similarities and connections between different types of information. It makes students engage actively with information, manipulating it rather than merely looking at it. And if you put the information on cards so that students can move the pieces around, it can give students who like to learn in tactile ways something to 'play' with.

## Tricks of the trade

Matching is a fairly basic information processing task so it really does need linking to additional activity to give it some bite. It's best used to get the ball rolling on a theme, or as a revision activity.

## Variations on a theme

- Remember playing find the pairs as a child? For an extra level of challenge, make students turn the cards over and find matching pairs. Much quieter than snap…

- Why stick to pairs and trios? Adapt 'Happy Families' to have students finding sets of four items of information. Four quotations from Macbeth, four from Lady Macbeth, four from Banquo, etc. Playing cards in class is always a winner…

- Save yourself the prep and get students making up domino sets or sets of happy families cards for revision. They'll learn twice in the process. Get the design and technology teacher to give you a hand and you've got a nice cross-curricular project to notch on your bedpost.

## Whizzing it

An easy one for your interactive whiteboard. Loads of Teachit Flash resources available, or use text boxes in Word to create your own simple electronic card sort.

# Mind maps

How to do them properly

## The basic idea

Easy to dismiss this as another 'magic bullet' fad because of all the hype that has periodically surrounded it, but a good solid technique nonetheless. Students take a large sheet of paper. They write or draw the central concept in the middle of the page. Then, using colours, lines, shapes and key words of their choice, they map their understanding of it to produce a diagram which clearly shows all the connections between the parts of their understanding. Isn't it just a spidergram? Well, it's related, but only in the same way that a sketch map on the back of an envelope is related to an Ordnance Survey map. Think OS here…

For the 'magic bullet' description of the registered trademark 'Mind Mapping' experience, visit **www.mind-mapping.co.uk**. The language is adult-oriented but it gives a comprehensive overview of what to do and why. Many more student-friendly versions can be found by talking to Mr Google.

## Applying it

- Use it to review a topic or theme when you think you've finished it, to check what students have got and what they haven't. Fill in missing bits and save for later revision purposes. Also use it straight for revision.

- Get students using it as a technique for making notes from texts they need to read. Because it relies on key words and images, it helps to get round the age old problem of students just copying out great chunks of text. It demands thought, but because it involves felt tipped pens students tend to engage with it more willingly.

- Works well for essay planning. If this needs building up, get them covering their page first, and then show how to add details, group things together, etc. Worth doing one together on the board. Bonus if you have an interactive whiteboard and can save and print.

## What's the point?

It gets students away from thinking in straight lines, supporting a more natural flow of ideas and encouraging creative connections to be made. Using colour, line and shape makes a nice change for everyone, and that new thinking space can free up fresh ideas. Students who like to 'see' ideas will be very happy, and there will usually be at least one student who stuns you with the depth and creativity that they can express in this format that is beyond them in conventional forms. Get your G&T talent spotter in when you're doing this. The visual dimension often means that the finished products are very memorable, making them excellent for open evening and for revision.

## Tricks of the trade

It's much harder than it looks. Students (and your head of department scowling through the door) think they are getting a nice kicked-back colouring-in lesson, but they soon realise you are actually evil and this takes considerable thought.

Especially if you keep pushing them to make properly labelled connections, to distinguish graphically between the significance of different ideas, and to keep adding layers until it really is Ordnance Survey grade. It's important to do that – this is no colouring-in lesson for you either – otherwise you'll get the entirely disposable back of the envelope sketch map. Because it's harder than it looks, try building up to it gradually, doing one as a class early on in the course, then group ones the next term, and finally individual ones. To do group ones effectively, use flipchart paper for size and give everyone a marker pen so they can all write simultaneously, adding new ideas, branching out from their own or other people's, etc. Otherwise it'll just be one person's mind map.

## Variations on a theme

- Give students a half-baked mind map and get them to add to it. This can be used as an activity in its own right, or to give some students more support, or to give all students support when they're first getting used to it.

## Whizzing it

Do it on your interactive whiteboard using standard drawing tools. Students can do likewise on PCs. Nothing fancier is necessary although there are various bits of mind mapping software available commercially and as shareware. But then you've got to teach students two things…

# Models

3D concept building not skinny girls on catwalks

## The basic idea

A big box of creative resources: whatever you can lay your hands on. Students then create three dimensional set designs for a scene, models of settings, mobiles (those hanging things, not the phones…) to represent abstract ideas, models to show the shape of the plot structure, and whatever else you can dream up.

## Applying it

- With one of the quirkiest Teachit resources (and therefore one of my personal favourites), have a go at creating Point Example Explanation mobiles to represent ideas about a text: **Key Stage 4>Skills>Reading skills>PEE mobile**.

- Set design for any play. Take one cardboard box and see what happens…

- Try making mobiles of poems: what shapes and colours and connections will they choose to represent the poem, or its different stanzas?. How can they represent the mood? Or different voices? That'll liven up your anthology a bit.

- Models work well in developing more sophisticated ideas about the function of the settings in all those split location Shakespeares: *The Winter's Tale, A Midsummer Night's Dream, Othello.* On the same basis at AS/A2 *A Room With A View, Wuthering Heights, Heart of Darkness…*

## What's the point?

It makes tangible students' understanding of text or topic so that differences of interpretation can be explored. As a three dimensional activity, it works best with things that have a distinct form or shape: settings, plot structures, and structured relationships between ideas. The practical task encourages creative expression and lots of discussion, and can be excellent for the development of teamwork as different students will have very different skills and strengths that will be useful.

### Tricks of the trade

Have plenty of interesting and unusual resources to inspire students and enable them to produce something impressive. Egg boxes and yogurt pots simply won't do it. You will need to prepare your room, with tables configured to allow practical group work – or beg a swap with Art or D&T when they need a row of desks for a change. Set and keep to a strict time limit, with a good ten to fifteen minutes of clearing up time at the end so that it's not you landed with the mess as the bell rings and another teacher comes flying into the room.

### Variations on a theme

- This is an ideal opportunity for some interesting group dynamics. Mix students up to create mini melting pots of very different learning styles, and invite evaluation of the process at the end. Try allocating one observer to each group with a formal role to assist in this evaluation by recording what happens.

### Whizzing it

The whole point is some hands on tactile action. Clicking a mouse just isn't the same.

# Music

Creative thinking around the text

## The basic idea

Students listen to music, produced in the same cultural context as the literary work, in order to explore similar veins of creative and artistic thought. Or they listen to music produced to accompany the text in some way, or as creative expression of it. They find or make music that would serve well as a soundtrack to the text.

### Applying it

- Get students listening to the music pieces mentioned in *Starseeker*, to compare their own responses with those described in the book.

- Get students critically analysing the soundtrack of an existing adaptation of the text before suggesting improvements. Especially good with really cheesy old versions ripe for a musical update. Or do it the other way round. Use to beef up Director's notes activities.

- Use music to explore cultural context and/or shamelessly indulge your own musical youth. My special contribution was 'Ghost Town' by The Specials and 'Walls Come Tumbling Down' by The Style Council to help A Level students understand the 1980s context of *Talking Heads*. A lesson never forgotten… Almost certainly for reasons involving far too much debate of my dancing style...

- For any poem called a song, get some of your talented musicians writing and performing the music. What style will they choose? Blake's 'Songs of Innocence and Experience', Donne's 'Songs', Eliot's 'The Love Song of J. Alfred Prufrock' and 'Rhapsody on a Windy Night'. Or try listening to someone else's compositions, such as John Taverner's renditions of Blake's 'The Lamb' and 'The Tyger'.

### What's the point?

It encourages students to think in a different way about their interpretation of a text, in a form that they are all highly familiar with from TV and film, and for musically minded students, it's a treat of a lesson. It makes real the decision about what kind of cultural context a production could be set in: will students go for music authentic to the period, or go for something much more urban and contemporary? It can open up really exciting and sharply contrasting interpretations that will spark lively debate because young people are often very passionate and articulate about their musical preferences.

### Tricks of the trade

Get a big stereo and play it loud some day when your classroom neighbours are out. Otherwise students will only spend half the lesson begging you to crank it up and not concentrating at all on the task. The walls really did nearly come tumbling down, but that may just have been my head of department pounding his fists on them in despair at my vernacular taste. Or trade a swap with a music teacher who wants to do essay writing for a change, or is at the Albert Hall for the afternoon with the brass section.

### Variations on a theme

- Go the whole hog and get students writing and producing the musical version of the text. I've seen them all: Rock'n'roll *A Midsummer Night's Dream*, bilingual power ballads in an adaptation of *A Tale of Two Cities*, and even the *Play Away* singalong version of *The Hungry Caterpillar*. All fantastic. Extra-curricular, obviously.

### Whizzing it

Multimedia animations with music, images, readings and text all coming together in a perfect harmony. Trust me, the students will know how to do it…

# Networking

Mapping the connectons between people and characters

## The basic idea

Sociologists and anthropologists (and some sociolinguists) use network diagrams to show patterns of social connection between people. Take this basic idea, some big sheets of paper, lots of felt tip pens, and get students producing their own models of the social worlds they encounter in life or fiction.

## Applying it (far easier to show than to tell!)

- For a simple version, use a radial diagram (in *Word>Insert>Diagram> Radial Diagram*). Put a character at the centre of the diagram, such as Nigel Hinton's Buddy, and the other characters in the radial blobs, and use the connecting lines to describe his feelings about each of them.

- Opposite is the start of a network diagram for *Romeo and Juliet*, a play with a complex social world that is a major factor in the action. For *Romeo and Juliet*, does this starter for ten match students' own perceptions of how the social network works? Add in the rest of the characters. Explore how the social world gradually closes in during the course of the play. Works well with any text where there are subtle connections and unexpected allegiances as drawing the diagram will involve lots of discussion and interesting variations.

- Can also be used very successfully at AS/A2 to get students discussing the connection between their individual coursework projects. They start with their own name in the middle and add blobs and spokes to show who connects and how – by theme or text, by approach or method. They then identify who is closest in the class network, and who it might be most useful to share ideas and problems with.

## What's the point?

It can draw out patterns and connections that a more linear approach to a text or situation can overlook. By making ideas visual, many students will find it easier to 'see' what is happening, and the active process of constructing the diagram will involve lots of discussion of different interpretations.

## Tricks of the trade

This is likely to be an unfamiliar approach to students, so it is probably best to show them what you mean first. You could try starting it off by getting them to draw their own social networks. This in itself might give rise to some useful starting points for autobiographical writing. Encourage students to experiment with creative ways of showing different kinds of connection, using colour, thickness of line, different patterns etc. After that, it's all about your skill in using question and answer to draw out the patterns and ideas that emerge from it.

### Variations on a theme

- If the full monty is a challenge too far, especially the first time they come across this, or you're in a race against time, try giving students a half-created network diagram to add to.

### Whizzing it

If you have a stack of blobs and lines at the ready, this is an easy one for whole class discussion and shared creation using the interactive whiteboard. Or go mad and create blobs with character's faces on for a souped up visually appealing version. Nothing wrong with a good old fashioned blob, mind…

# The social world of Romeo and Juliet

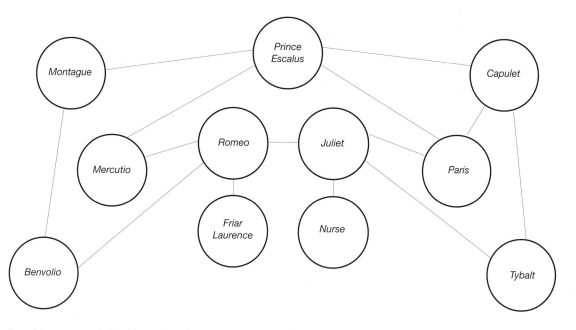

(a work in progress: relationships and reactions need noting on the lines)

# News desk

Sleaze and scandal - read all about it!

## The basic idea

Students produce news stories or a whole newspaper based on the text being studied. They research and write different types of news and feature articles based on characters, themes, settings, plot incidents, features of social and historical context. Red top shock horror or black top chatter. Disaster reports with eye witness reports and scene of the crime diagrams; agony aunt advice; travel features; obituaries. Endless possibilities.

## Applying it

• Working on *Holes*? Get students producing newspaper coverage of the Kissin' Kate scandal in Teachit's **Key Stage 3>Prose>Holes by Louis Sachar>Green Lake Informer**. Or the *Inverness Chronicle* the day after Duncan's murder in **Key Stage 3>Drama>Macbeth>Macbeth: The murder**.

• For a whole newspaper, any text with an unfamiliar historical or geographical setting works well: at Key Stage 4 try it with *To Kill A Mockingbird*; also works every time as a starting point for Chaucer. Tried, tested, and Encarta-friendly topics include: pilgrims and pilgrimages; courtly love; Medieval Britain; chivalry; Chaucer; the Crusades; Medieval science; Medieval occupations.

• For a bit of variation, have different groups of students producing newspapers with different political allegiances, or different editorial policies, presenting the same stories from their biased perspective. Try the events of *Romeo and Juliet* as seen by the *Montague Mercury* and the *Capulet Courier* (rubbish titles, I agree...). Try a sleazy tabloid version of events from *Lord of the Flies* versus some high-minded we're-still-a-broadsheet-honest version.

### What's the point?

It can be a fun way of researching and developing ideas about social or historical context, or a lively way of exploring different interpretations of the text. Working together in groups or as a class to produce a whole newspaper gives students the opportunity to exercise complex teamwork and collaboration skills, especially if you model a formal editorial process. Appointing editors is a nice way of nurturing leadership talent.

### Tricks of the trade

Set definite parameters for the task. Only allow a certain number of pages as this keeps the task from spiralling out of control, is more realistic, and requires sharper editorial decisions and redrafting. The front page can be quite enough with some classes. Requiring the use of a template saves time that might otherwise be wasted in agonising over layout and font.

### Variations on a theme

• Tie it in with a visit to a local newspaper.

• Differentiate by helping all students to pick topics and tasks that fire their imagination, challenging stronger ones to tackle more demanding or unfamiliar types of news writing, and encouraging different ways of completing the task.

• To speed it up, reduce the number of pages needed and set tighter content guidelines. You could also provide information packs for students to work from rather than letting them enter the strange mutating time zone that is the internet. Have fun being the draconian chief of a news desk with a rapidly approaching deadline by which time the paper must go to press or they're all fired. (I like this version a LOT!)

• To slow it down, set it up as an extended process of research, writing, editorial meetings, redrafting, all building up to eventual publication. Give students distinct roles so that the meetings develop a life and an agenda of their own.

### Whizzing it

This certainly used to be done with black sugar paper and a glue stick, but it's hard to imagine it being done in any other way now than with all the techno-wizardry of a PC suite. Glory in the wonder... Electronic templates are available from Teachit if you or your school/college are subscribers, and/or try the Microsoft Office newsletter templates page at **http://office.microsoft.com**

# News wall

Classroom walls papered for free (just don't let the caretaker see)

## The basic idea

You clear lots of space on one of your classroom walls or noticeboards. Start it off with a really interesting newspaper or magazine article that is related in some way to what you are doing. For a certain period every student is charged with the task of adding at least one thing to the news wall.

### Applying it

- Set up a general news wall, such as an English Language or English Literature news wall.

- Set up a specific news wall that relates to where you are in your scheme of work, such as a Shakespeare news wall (he's never out of the news, that bloke) or a dialect news wall (likewise).

### What's the point?

It encourages students to explore the connections between the world of the classroom and the world outside. This can really motivate some students, and is useful for everyone in bringing fresh ideas and perspectives into the classroom. It also means you have a five minute activity any time you need a change of focus, or a starting point – just get the student to introduce their article and tease out what is interesting about it. It also demands wider reading in a relatively undemanding way, encouraging a shift towards greater independence.

### Tricks of the trade

It can be useful to enlarge the articles rather than just sticking them on the wall, as this encourages students to actually read what's up there. Make time every now and again for students to do just that, giving them a week to nominate their favourite piece so far, for example. Sometimes it's the simplest things that get in the way of students reading the news wall, like a desk, so make sure it's in a space where circulation is possible. You generally need to be a bit assertive about this activity to get it going, but once students get on a roll you can end up wallpapering your whole classroom. Lead from the front at first, bringing in things you have found and telling them where you found them. Make sure they are from the popular media to start off with, not the *Times Ed*. Gives you an excuse to read *Chat!* and *FHM* anyway…

### Variations on a theme

- Rather than setting this task over a long period, you could set it as a one-off, giving students a week to find an article for the board. To avoid copying, offer cool prizes for everyone who finds something no-one else has got.

- Set different students different challenges. Some students might get carte blanche, some might be challenged to find an extended article of so many words, or to use the more serious newspapers or magazines.

### Whizzing it

Set up a shared blog with students as contributors. Then their task is each to write a post at some point in the set period with a hyperlink to their article in electronic form. This is deep joy for a lot of students, and you get the side bonus that to become a team blogger they have to start their own individual blog (see **Journals** on page 65) and anything that encourages them to write for the fun of it has to be good.

# Ninety second versions
## Reassuringly difficult

## The basic idea

Take any kind of text you like as long as it takes considerably more then ninety seconds to read. Students produce and then read or perform the ninety second version. The challenge is to produce a version that is both brief and retains as much of the essence of the full text as possible.

### Applying it

• Anything a bit spooky can be great fun – Robert Louis Stevenson's *The Body Snatcher* works well, try also Edgar Allen Poe's *The Tell Tale Heart*. Copies available in Teachit's **Key Stage 3/4>Prose>Teachit's short story library**.

• Use as a post-reading comprehension check. With more time, add in discussion of what happens when you abridge a text. Can help get over the 'why is this book so long...' wailing from the back of the class by throwing the question back at 'em.

• The Reduced Shakespeare Company have made a tidy living out of this kind of activity. How about a Reduced *The Arabian Nights*, with each student doing a ninety second version of one of the tales?

• Get students producing a ninety second revision version of the dreaded GCSE anthology. Ninety seconds is quite enough of that for anyone, though when my churlish A Level class claimed their ninety second versions of Keats' narrative poems were a major improvement on the originals, I wept. So young and so untender...

### What's the point?

It's harder than students think it will be! It requires careful reading of the text, then precise and judicious selection of the key elements needed to keep the story hanging together. If the reading/performance is to move beyond plot paraphrase, students have to use language creatively in the style of the author to evoke mood and character, to realise settings and their significance, to be clear about narrative point of view and author's attitude, to give us a taste of the dialogue. Everything, indeed, that constitutes a text, but concentrated into a sparkling miniature.

### Tricks of the trade

You need to explain the task carefully so that students understand it as a miniature of the original not as a simplistic paraphrase. Get them first brainstorming the constituent components of a novel – according to the level at which you are working – so that they have a tick-list of things they need to include.

### Variations on a theme

• Check out *One Hundred Novels in Haiku* by David Bader for an even more demanding version – genius at work and a book for the wish list you give your class at the start of the academic year for all gifting occasions.

• Check out 'The Digested Read' (with additional 'The digested read, digested' feature) in the books section of the *Guardian* available online at **http://books.guardian.co.uk**. There's a task for original writing with a real purpose.

### Whizzing it

Ninety second versions are ideal material for short animations using Flash or PowerPoint. Great for showing off at open evening.

# Noughts and crosses

One of the simple pleasures in life

## The basic idea

Take a topic for revision and two warring opponents. Draw a noughts and crosses grid on the board. First opponent selects a square and has to answer a question on the topic correctly. If s/he does, they can put their marker in the square; if not, they can't. First one to get a straight line through three squares, vertically, horizontally or diagonally.

### Applying it

• Livens up work on accurate recognition of word classes at Key Stage 3, or when you are tired of beating your AS English Language students up for having forgotten everything they ever learned at Key Stage 3.

• Practise accurate punctuation skills. Give students a short text or a series of sentences with missing punctuation to work on. If you have an IWB, flash it up on the big screen. Play the game, with correct identification winning squares.

• Try flashing up quotations for students to identify who said what and why, or true/false statements about the text, or full on quiz questions that require thorough understanding and explanation.

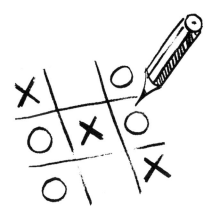

### What's the point?

It's nothing fancy, but revision is a deeply tedious affair and livening it up with a game can help create a more lively dynamic that is more conducive to learning. A bit of healthy competition can be useful in that context as it will tend to encourage quicker thinking under pressure, as the opposition sit there busting a gut going 'Miss, miss, I know the answer, me, me!'

### Tricks of the trade

Think about how you can set it up so that everyone stays engaged. No slackers having a nap at the back. Try teams. Try pairs. Try winner stays on. Try doing it in small groups, with two opponents and a question master, swapping roles in three rounds so everyone does everything. Better to do it in short bursts each lesson than one humungous great session as the novelty can wear off quite quickly.

### Variations on a theme

• Save yourself the preparation and get students writing the questions – it'll be far better for their learning. Besides, students always love creating fiendish questions to test others with. You can always throw a few bonus ones in as the session progresses.

• Use it as a five-minute-wonder-spot at the start or end of a lesson to keep everyone on their toes, and to check who is actually doing any revision as the weeks leading up to the exams tick by.

• Have different questions prepared so you can give different students different levels of challenge. No need to make it obvious.

### Whizzing it

Easy opportunity to show off your interactive whiteboard. Have the grid and piles of coloured shapes stacked up in a Word document and off you go.

# Obstacle race

Finding information with your pants on fire

## The basic idea

Students have to find specified types of information as fast as they can. Flat races are good, but so are those with hurdles and obstacles and ditches and water jumps. Metaphorically speaking.

## Applying it

- Get students racing against each other to find words in dictionaries as in Teachit's resource *Key Stage 3>Skills>Dictionary and thesaurus skills>Dictionary and scanning race*.

- Soup up existing research tasks with a bit of competitive spice. Teachit's *Key Stage 3/4/5>Genre>An introduction to writers and their times>-the canon of English Literature* would work well like this.

- It's a good technique for introducing students to different resources in the library or the learning centre. Not that your librarian will necessarily agree with you but if you get him/her/them involved it can be a beautiful bonding opportunity.

- Race to find page and line references to complete a set of notes about a character. Could be used with any text, but very nicely demonstrated in Teachit's *The Winter's Tale* resource *Key Stage 5>Drama>The Winter's Tale>Leontes: a character sheet*.

## What's the point?

It gets simple information gathering tasks done speedily and with focused attention. It practises rapid reading processes like skimming and scanning. The competitive edge can generate a bit of a buzz, especially if there's a brand new Mini Cooper as the prize for finishing first. It's not a fancy technique but it makes a change.

### Tricks of the trade

Insist on the accuracy of the information gathered and test that whatever sources you are going to use are actually useful and accessible. Otherwise frustration sets in and some students give up. Whilst pushing through may very well be a useful learning experience, it's not always desirable so do the prep.

### Variations on a theme

- Create different challenges for different students: less time, less information about where to look, more complex information to find, no internet access.

### Whizzing it

Race to find specified information about any topic with some students only using the internet and some students only using traditional resources. Great for comparing the value of the two sources, as in Teachit's *Language library>Language variation>A race against time*, where students find information about key dialect studies. The internet always wins but it still generates very healthy discussion about some of the limitations of the web. Easily adapted for other topics.

# Odd one out

A cunning little activity to keep 'em guessing

## The basic idea

Give the students four poems, four pictures, four objects, four anything you can think ofs... Three have something in common, one is the odd one out. Students discuss the items and decide which is which, then explain and justify their choices.

### Applying it

• Use to develop storytelling. Three objects belong to one story, one doesn't. Which, why, what story? Nice as a free-standing imaginative writing task, very nice if you then lead into reading a story with the three objects in it. Try it with objects from 'The Adventure of the Speckled Band' by Arthur Conan Doyle.

• Take four texts from an anthology, students to decide which one has the least connection to the other three, either free-standing or in relation to a particular question or theme. Good for practising selection of texts.

• Works well to test out students' understanding of a writer's style. As an example, take two Gillian Clarke poems from the anthology, one of her poems not in the anthology and one by another poet in a similar vein. Good for revision too.

### What's the point?

It can help to foster effective discrimination, requiring as it does careful attention to detail, consideration of similarities and differences, and lateral and/or creative thinking about possibilities. Students with a problem-solving disposition are likely to enjoy solving the puzzle.

### Tricks of the trade

The trick lies in choosing items where either there isn't a correct answer or it's not obvious. Otherwise the activity gets finished in three minutes flat and you end up wishing you hadn't spent an hour preparing all the materials for it. Use good questioning that probes and interrogates beneath the surface answer to help students develop fuller justification of their ideas. It's the dialogue and discussion that matters not the puzzle itself.

### Variations on a theme

• Give different students different odd one out puzzles to work on to allow for different levels of interest or ability. Different sets of texts, different amounts of text to deal with, different complexity of ideas or style.

• Get students preparing their own puzzle sets to test other students with as a revision activity.

• Can be used as a quick starter to lead into discussion or other activity; to extend it, have a series of related puzzles for students to work on, or add another text and another to test the boundaries of the category, or build up to formal comparative essay writing.

### Whizzing it

Do it *A Question of Sport* style on the big IWB screen for a whole class focus, or team quiz. For revision have four texts picked randomly from the anthology with teams competing to give the best answer – have a panel of judges to decide.

# Opinion cards
## Ways of eliciiting higher quality critical opinions

## The basic idea

Make up sets of cards representing certain types of opinion. Students are given one or more of the cards and have to formulate a response within this constraint. Use in small group discussion or whole class. Holding them up provides an instant straw poll, beating a 'hands up' approach because everyone does it more or less simultaneously, giving individuals less room to change an answer merely to be part of the dominant group. Hundreds of variations but here are a few:

## Applying it

• Give each student or pair one complete set of cards. In whole class feedback of a discussion on any topic or text they choose which one they would most like to 'play' to determine their contribution. Beats vague rambling feedback any day.

• With the coloured dots or playing cards, 'deal' them out, one per student, and they are constrained to give only the type of opinion on their card. Any topic, any text.

• Numbered cards and TUF cards (see below) very useful for taking a straw poll at the start of a debate or discussion or investigation on any topic: students simply hold them up and you count. Test again half way through, and again at the end. Explore what happened, what caused people to change their minds, etc.

• The playing cards set of descriptors is useful as a starter for review writing where everyone has read the same book.

## What's the point?

It can get discussion started, especially if you have classes of diffident students or at the start of a course when they're a bit shy with each other. Sometimes, they just don't know what they are 'supposed' to say and this gives them prompts which over time they may internalise. The numbered cards force students to commit to a position, which can be helpful, while the TUF cards can be used in factual circumstances to give you an instant assessment of who has understood what.

## Tricks of the trade

Make the cards aesthetically satisfying objects that they want to play with: coloured laminated star cards never last long in my classroom… Apart from that design consideration, keep it snappy and politely insist on a response, offering to come back to that student later if they are not ready. Don't leave it to the end, though, as they may be banking on all other ideas being expressed so they can just say 'everyone's already said what I was thinking'. Surprise them by asking them two goes later, or five, or whatever. This sends out the important message that there is no cop-out in your classroom. And if they insist that their opinion has already been expressed, give them a follow-up question that probes it deeper. No cop-outs.

### Variations on a theme

• I'm especially fond of Blu-Tacking the card under their seat so they first have to find it but I think there is therapy available for this…

• Stack the deck so that you deal certain types of cards to individuals you want to challenge in a particular way. The carte blanche option can be good for stronger students, but try also giving the positive card to your biggest whinger who thinks everything is rubbish, and the negative card to your sunny optimist.

• Forget the categories and just use the cards as a random method for dividing students into different kinds of groups; or do this and then get each group working on a particular type of response together.

# Whizzing it

Have the cards set up as text boxes in a Word document, formatted to go behind any other text box. Also have a rubbish bin in a text box in the document. Whack it all up on the interactive whiteboard. Get each student to pick a card, give their response and then throw their card in the rubbish bin where it will magically disappear. Only have a set number of each type of card so that as you progress round the class the task increases in tension and students start begging to let you go next so they get their pick.

| Coloured dot or star cards | purple | = | positive or supportive opinion |
| | red | = | negative or opposing opinion |
| | green | = | new idea or line of enquiry sparked |
| | orange | = | any other opinion or argument |
| Playing cards | diamond | = | aspect most enjoyed |
| | ace | = | aspect most challenged by |
| | heart | = | question you'd most like to ask the author |
| | club | = | any other comment |
| Numbered cards 1-5 | 1 | = | strongly agree |
| | 5 | = | strongly disagree |
| T U F cards | T for True, U for Unsure, F for False | | |

# Order from chaos

Classification activities to soothe the soul

## The basic idea

Give students a pile of stuff – words, texts, books, whatever – and get them organising this into specific groups. You might tell them what groups to sort it into, you might get them to determine their own groups, according to your purpose. At the end, what appeared to be a chaotic heap of random knowledge is neatly ordered and under analytical control. Well, except that as in Shakespeare's comedies, a good classification task will always leave one character who doesn't quite fit the happy mould, just to keep it real.

### Applying it

• Classify characters according to type or function. In Teachit's **Key Stage 3>Prose>Harry Potter and the Philosopher's Stone by J.K. Rowling>Part 1 tasks**, characters have to be put in the right house. A quick and easy classification question.

• Give students a big pile of texts and get them to sort them into different types of writing: explain, describe, narrate, explore, analyse, imagine, discuss, argue, persuade. Give them criteria first or use existing understanding and deduce the fine detail afterwards.

• Give them a pile of words to classify according to word class. Lots of cross boundary issues for lively debate that will run for weeks. Try Teachit's Flash activity that has students classifying nouns and verbs **Key Stage 3>Skills>Sentence level work>Nouns and verbs**. AS English Language students may need this too!

### What's the point?

Classification is an important skill for being able to handle large bodies of knowledge, so it is important that students develop it, recognise it as a useful tool, and in later stages of their education develop a critical perspective on it. It requires precise discrimination, the ability to conceptualise differences, and a sensitive appreciation of cross-boundary issues (the ones that overlap or don't fit anywhere). And quite apart from all the academic justification, it's a useful life skill for sock drawers, CD racks and tool boxes.

### Tricks of the trade

Don't skimp on the number of resources provided: this is actually easier to do with a bigger pile than a smaller one as there will be more connections and possibilities. But do keep the amount of text relatively small, as you want the focus to be on the categories of knowledge and brain kernels start popping out of the pan if they've got to process large texts too.

### Variations on a theme

• Students are always complaining that they don't know how to find anything in the library. So give them a project to investigate existing classification systems, devise a better one, and write formal reports or give presentations to the library staff. Student Voice rocks – as does a real context for writing. Look at **www.cool-reads.co.uk** for an example of how the young teenage lads who created this site have classified fiction.

• The reverse version of this activity is **Odd one out** (page 93). Combine the two by getting students to complete a classification task. At exactly the point when they're feeling a warm smug glow of intellectual satisfaction, give them a 'spanner in the works' text which may or may not be an odd one out. Mean? It's good for 'em!

### Whizzing it

Put the items to be classified into text boxes so you can do the answers on the interactive whiteboard, moving them into the right positions in your classification system. Nothing fancy but provides a big focal point. Especially if you use nice colours…

# The play's the thing

Bring out your inner Hollywood/Bollywood, RSC/London Palladium

## The basic idea

Students engage in the production of a performance – of the full unexpurgated version of a dramatic text, an abridgement, adaptation or extract. Published, unpublished, improvised. With or without props, sets or costumes according to time, resources and inclination. Size/composition of audience according to logistics and aspirations.

### Applying it

- For a rich range of activities that could be used as the foundation for performances of several key scenes from *Romeo and Juliet*, including the fight scene, check out Teachit's **Key Stage 3>Drama>Romeo and Juliet Drama unit>Scheme of work – Romeo & Juliet**. Likewise for *Macbeth* **Key Stage 3/4>Drama> Macbeth: a Drama scheme>Drama scheme of work focusing on Act 1 Scene 1**.

- Get groups of students to select and work on a performance of different *Talking Heads* monologues and then write their own.

- Try it with a *Shakespeare in a Box* set, everything you need to stage a 45 minute mini-production in no time at all. Available in *Taming of the Shrew* or *King Lear* flavours, the latter complete with fake eyeball and plastic dagger. Published by Workman Publishing Company.

- As a pre-reading task, do before and after scenes to develop discussion e.g. *Othello* Act 2 Scene 1 'O, my fair warrior!' dialogue, and Act 5 Scene 2 lines 1-85.

### What's the point?

This kind of activity is very rich in all kinds of points, but essentially it is about enabling students to experience a dramatic situation from the inside. It can encourage close readings of the text or other source material, and can bring out alternative readings in a very tangible way. It encourages all the teamwork skills of negotiation and collaboration, and allows students with talents in performance, leadership and the visual realisation of ideas to shine. Improvisation work, both as a pre-reading task and in response to key moments, gives students an opportunity to explore their own experiences, attitudes and ideas which can help to make subsequent discussion of the text or original writing much richer.

### Tricks of the trade

Allocate production and performance roles, so that everyone has a part to play, different strengths and skills are valued and developed, and to ensure that someone is keeping an eye on time management and quality. Don't hog all the best roles.

### Variations on a theme

- Get different groups of students to produce different kinds of performance of the same scene, e.g. ones with different historical settings.

- Task students with keeping a production diary in paper or electronic format (try blogging). Conclude with peer evaluation of group work and diaries.

### Whizzing it

Go on location with digital video cameras to film a scene of the play. My disgruntled GCSE retake boys produced great versions of the dagger scene of *Macbeth* on location at a local castle.

# Postcards home

Those Martians trying to make sense of human life

## The basic idea

Look at a familiar theme, issue or experience from an unfamiliar point of view, as in Craig Raine's poem, 'A Martian Sends A Postcard Home'. Useful as a stimulus for imaginative writing and for establishing pre-reading perspectives on key themes. These can then be compared and contrasted with those encountered in the text.

### Applying it

• Using May Swenson's poem Teachit's resource **Key Stage 3>Poetry>An introduction to poetry> 'Southbound on the Freeway'** has students role playing aliens (not a hard task, then…) and broadcasting their experiences of Earth back home.

• Continuing the alien theme, Teachit's **Key Stage 3>Poetry>Poetry basics>Poem into the future** has students exploring what it is to be human and writing poems for future inhabitants of outer space

• Lots of possibilities at all stages for original writing in the style of, and for text transformation, developing the Raine poem into a short story, drama, epistolary novel, etc.

• Before studying the love poems of John Donne, or indeed any collection of love poems, or any text with love as a central theme, explore the conceit of the Raine poem, collect 21st century cultural products that show ideas about love and write Martian poems on this theme.

### What's the point?

This technique is particularly useful when students take for granted their own and/or common attitudes and assumptions about some aspect of human experience. Getting students to identify the cultural specificity of these attitudes and assumptions is a valuable activity in its own right, as well as being of great value to the exploration of alternative literary interpretations. It encourages problem solving, lateral thinking and creativity in thought and literary production.

### Tricks of the trade

Allow plenty of time for students to figure out the metaphors in the Raine poem, and don't give them any clues unless absolutely necessary! Draw out the effects of this style of writing, and its

purpose, otherwise students can end up just trying to create a fiendishly cryptic crossword, rather than producing any fresh or original perspectives on the theme.

### Variations on a theme

• To speed this up, give students a mini-anthology of cultural products to work with rather than them researching their own. To save you researching them too, check out the list of love poems on page 19 of the Teachit resource **Key Stage 5>Prose>Wuthering Heights by Emily Bronte>A comprehensive study pack**. Don't be put off by the *Wuthering Heights* connection: it's a well-designed generic pre-teaching activity about love that could be used in all sorts of contexts.

• To slow it down, work on a whole exhibition of 21st century cultural products, original poems and thematic comparisons with the text.

• Differentiation can be served by giving students different cultural products to work with, or a different range. Give strong students more challenging texts and/or more complex and ambiguous representations of the theme.

• For more creative extension, find or create, or get students to find or create, a real publication context for the best of their poems or other original writing.

### Whizzing it

Get students to create multimedia animated versions of the poems explored and/or created (especially if you've got an open evening coming up). Or set up a class blog or similar shared online resource. Invite students to submit cultural products there, in text, image, video or hyperlink form, with an explanation of their choices. Encourage online discussion of these. Join in with questions and suggestions as appropriate.

# Posters

Ahh, kick back and drink tea lesson (in your dreams, anyway...)

## The basic idea

Scissors, glue, sugar paper, good felt tipped pens and a box of magazines for those of a collage persuasion. Pick a topic. Students work individually, in pairs, or in groups to produce a poster showing their ideas or interpretations. The work is presented to the rest of the class.

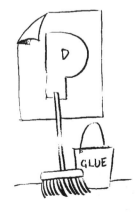

### Applying it

- Wanted posters for villains as in Teachit's *Key Stage 3>Prose>Oliver Twist (NLS Y8) by Charles Dickens> Wanted poster* which has students designing wanted posters for Fagin and the Artful Dodger. Likewise Teachit's *Key Stage 3>Prose>I Am David by Anne Holm>What does David look like?* Nice…

- Posters for productions of plays or film adaptations as in Teachit's *Key Stage 3>Prose>Holes by Louis Sachar> Holes (The movie)*.

- Posters exploring issues as a pre-reading task, as in Teachit's resource which gets students creating collages about culture and traditions *Key Stage 4>Poetry>Poems from different cultures>Pre-teaching collage activity*.

- Educational wallcharts on contextual topics e.g. Gothic literature.

- Visual representations of contrasting settings such as Thrushcross Grange and Wuthering Heights, or the different places Gulliver travels to.

### What's the point?

Ignore anyone who harrumphs when they see you walking down the corridor with your box of tricks. At its most limited, this technique is a useful survival strategy, buying a bit of time when the lesson-planning pressure gets to you. Taking your foot off the pedal can also create valuable space for freer thinking and discussion, and for students to exercise creativity and independence. If worked on in groups, collaboration and discussion are encouraged. Visual and kinaesthetic learners are made very happy. It draws out and makes tangible where the students' thinking is at, in ideas and connections, in interpretations. It also requires them to commit to their ideas.

### Tricks of the trade

The trick is to make sure you have a classroom culture of high expectation, in which students understand that their task is to produce something striking and original in conception and execution. It is not just colouring in.

### Variations on a theme

- Students can be set the same task, e.g. all create a wanted poster for Macbeth and compare interpretations, or a part of a larger whole, e.g. each student produces a poster about one character for a wall mounted dramatis personae of the play.

- Presentation can be a simple matter of classroom display (especially useful if you have an open evening coming up) or formal oral presentation. If you have a large class this can get a bit tedious, so another option is to display the posters and have half the class going to look at them and half answering their questions about them.

- Strong students could be set poster tasks requiring greater breadth, depth, pace or expertise e.g. instead of a single character portrait from Chaucer's *The General Prologue to the Canterbury Tales*, create an interesting group of characters and represent them in a way that shows their connections.

- The quick version of this is a single lesson in which a poster is produced, displayed and discussed. The slow version can involve multiple lessons with poster production, presentation, discussion, comparison and evaluation all playing a part.

### Whizzing it

Throw out the sugar paper and get students to produce their posters using ICT. A more challenging version of this would be for them to produce a digital interactive 'poster' that could be projected onto an interactive whiteboard for other students to explore. This might include sound, images and hyperlinks but would still essentially be one 'sheet'.

# Predictions

All the what-iffy stuff

## The basic idea

Before reading a text, give students some fragments of it. The image from the book jacket. The title (unless it's something they all know and are already groaning about). The first line. A few alluring quotations. A few striking images. Any of these or all of these and whatever other kinds of fragments you fancy. Get the students figuring out as much as they can about what the book will be about: characters, themes, plot, settings, style, genre.

### Applying it

- Predict the middle of a text from the beginning and end as in Teachit's *Key Stage 3>Poetry>Ballads>'The Sad Story of Lefty and Ned' – predictions activity*.

- Predict what happens from a series of key events and the kind of ending as in Teachit's *Key Stage 3>Drama>Twelfth Night>Pre-teaching: Introductory activities, including predictions*.

- Use it to explore how writers sow the seeds of their endings in their beginnings, as in Teachit's thoroughly modelled resource *Key Stage 3>Skills>Story openings and endings(NLSY7)>Using clues to predict a story*. Focuses on a Graham Greene story.

- Give them key words and images from a poem, such as Blake's 'London' – 'charter'd', 'marks of weakness', 'mind-forg'd manacles', 'black'ning Church', 'youthful harlot' – and get them making predictions from there.

- Ignore the well-known title, *Big Brother* and *Room 101*, and get students speculating from the brilliant opening line of *1984*, a couple of the slogans, and 'Do it to Julia; do it to Julia'.

### What's the point?

It gets students thinking about the text actively before they start reading. This gives them a frame of reference rather than approaching it 'cold', and opens up useful lines of enquiry about their expectations which can then be tested and explored further as the reading progresses. It invites valuable wider discussion about how we read and how we form initial judgements. It gets students looking closely at small pieces of evidence and using inductive reasoning to piece together some ideas

about the text. Speculative thinking is creative; practised regularly it can eventually overcome any ingrained and unproductive 'just tell me the answer' thinking.

### Tricks of the trade

This works far better if you sneak the text up on the students without any fanfare or 'coming soon' trailers. If half of them have already started reading it, it won't work nearly as well. For that reason it can sometimes work more effectively with individual poems than with the set text heavyweights, but context is all here.

### Variations on a theme

- There is a way of still using this technique if students do have some prior knowledge of the text, though not necessarily having read it, e.g. they think they know all about *Romeo and Juliet* by playground osmosis. That is to give them an unexpected image from an 'alternative' production (all male actors, for example), and some of the more interesting but less well known lines. Get them speculating about what might be in the text that challenges their assumptions. That's good too, and can create a more open-minded start to the scheme of work.

- When you've finished studying the text, get students selecting a fragments package for the next year group. You'll have a brilliant set of teaching resources in no time.

### Whizzing it

Go big screen by dropping your fragments into PowerPoint and animating it. Let the showreel roll: students discuss and scribble down notes as the slides appear and disappear. Like on *University Challenge* when they play the bits of music. Add little audio or video clips if you want to get really swanky.

# Presentations

How to get decent ones

## The basic idea

Students prepare and give a formal presentation on some aspect of the topic or text being studied, individually or in collaboration with others, with or without fancy multimedia presentation tools.

### Applying it

- 'My hero' is a perennially popular option though do make it clear what you mean by heroism unless you actually want 'My favourite celebrity'. Though I quite like seeing who's in and who's not… Maybe I'll get my classroom sponsored by *Hello* magazine… Or get them presenting their ambitions as in Teachit's **Key Stage 3>Skills>Speaking and listening tasks>Ambitions talk**.

- Attach a 'real' presentation to study of a literary text, as in the presentations of a homelessness charity to the National Lottery Commission in Teachit's resource **Key Stage 3>Prose>Stone Cold by Robert Swindells>Speaking and Listening – Helping the homeless**.

- Presentation of research on the social and historical background to a text, as in Teachit's **Key Stage 4>Prose>Dr Jekyll and Mr Hyde>Dr Jekyll and Mr Hyde – research topics.** Likewise **Key Stage 4/5>Prose> Dracula by Bram Stoker>Research and presentation tasks**.

- At Advanced Level, presentation of an interpretation of a literary text from a specific theoretical point of view e.g. a feminist or Marxist or psychoanalytical account. Works wonderfully well with Henry James' *The Turn Of The Screw*.

### What's the point?

To encourage students to take responsibility for their own learning, and to develop confident and coherent oral communication skills. Group presentations present a nice complex teamwork task if students are challenged to think beyond a simple succession of three or four chunks of information. Use of multimedia presentation tools can allow students with good visual skills to shine, and usually encourages even the most timid/reluctant to have a go. There is also the wise old adage that learning doesn't come any better than when you have to teach it to someone else.

### Tricks of the trade

Presentation lessons look ridiculously easy but they are very deceptive. Good learning is far more likely to take place if careful thought goes into the task design. Skip this and nine times out of ten you will end up thinking the last however many lessons were a complete waste of time. So:

Don't set up individual presentations in a large class unless absolutely necessary because sitting through them all is worse than water torture. If they are necessary for assessment purposes, try to do a few at a time over a longer period.

*(continued over)*

Don't expect excellent presentations to happen automatically. They rely on a complex set of skills. Work with students on these, and on what standard you expect them to reach. The Key Skills standards for length and quality are actually quite a useful set of benchmarks.

If doing group presentations, set each a different task wherever possible, or make the task sufficiently open-ended that a good variety of outcome is probable. This avoids the crushing boredom of listening to six different versions of the same thing, and helps to encourage good comparative discussion.

Give listeners a specific role to keep them focused on other students' work. Making notes of comparisons with their own findings and others, having to think of one good question to ask, and summarising the three main points are all useful techniques.

Give students real audiences wherever possible, not just their classmates. Invite some guests from the community, a university or business; another class, older, younger, from another subject, or from another school/college; the head; their parents; whoever you can think of to challenge them to produce their very best work. Real purposes have a similar effect.

## Variations on a theme

• Vary the formats for presentation if you use this technique frequently, partly for variety's sake, partly to support the development of a wider repertoire of skills. Options might include variation of the size of the audience, degree of formality required, availability of different presentation tools, degree of conformity or creativity expected, venue, etc.

• Presentations can also draw on more creative talents. Making speeches in role as a character is one version of this. Getting students to create a stimulating presentation from their work on texts in an anthology is another. The more you loathe the anthology, the better the level of challenge!

• Try varying the length of presentation required. Talented orators may be much more challenged by being set less time.

• The slow version involves lessons spent planning, researching, drafting, rehearsing, presenting and evaluating; do it with information sources already smouldering and no fancy multimedia gizmos and you can do it from a standing start in an hour.

## Whizzing it

Help students develop their use of PowerPoint or other presentation tools. Encourage experimentation with digital image, video and audio files, if appropriate to the task; explore how design and animation features do or don't help the communication of the content. There's no point simply telling them to stop fiddling because it'll never happen!

# Prove it

Find evidence and test it to destruction - not for the faint-hearted

## The basic idea

Take one or more assertions and test them against the evidence. Use assertions made by authoritative figures in published sources, your own inventions, those made by past or present anonymous students, and/or by fictional characters. The more critical the interrogation of the evidence the better. Only those assertions that really stand up to interrogation should be left at the end. In this activity, rejection and destruction are valid critical and creative thought processes.

### Applying it

- Test statements made by characters about themselves e.g. Lear's 'I am a man more sinned against than sinning' or 'I am a very foolish fond old man' in Shakespeare's *King Lear*.

- Test assertions made by literary critics about texts as in Teachit's **Key Stage 5>Drama>Othello>Critical readings of Iago**, likewise also **Critical readings of Othello** in the same place.

- Testing and comparison of 12 student assertions about the language and style of *Captain Corelli's Mandolin* are at the heart of Teachit's resource **Key Stage 5>Prose>Captain Corelli's Mandolin by Louis de Bernières> The exorbitant auditory impediment**.

### What's the point?

This activity can help to develop close reading and critical thinking about the quality and quantity of evidence needed to provide effective substantiation of a line of argument. This is an important skill for academic forms of discourse, including essay writing and debate, and for working independently when faced with conflicting versions of the truth. It can be used to encourage students to examine a justifiable line of argument, regardless of whether they agree with it or not, and to develop their ability to actively reject ideas that don't pass muster. This can help to encourage intellectual commitment, confidence and flexibility.

### Tricks of the trade

Make the assertions sufficiently interesting, controversial, unusual or unexpected to make students want to bother trawling through sources of evidence. Give students the opportunity to select and reject from a wide range of assertions, including ones you consider completely unjustifiable, otherwise you are only asking them to provide standard proofs rather than exercising critical judgement and creative thought. Insist upon high standards of evidence, as appropriate to the student's level.

### Variations on a theme

- For greater extension, link this to work on literary theory, such as can be found in the English and Media Centre pack, *Text Reader Critic*. Another kind of extension would be to link this to work on the theory of knowledge, exploring how ideas in Language or Literature are developed.

- The quick version involves straightforward analysis of relevant evidence, and a decision on whether or not the assertion is justified. The slower version might involve cross-examination of each other's decisions, and presentation both of what has been accepted and which assertions were rejected and why.

# Pyramids

Building class discussion step by step

## The basic idea

A technique for engaging everyone in the class in discussion. You start with individual reflection or note-making on the question in hand; individuals then pair up to discuss their thoughts; then pairs form fours, fours form eights, and from there to whole class discussion unless you really want to get into sixteens.

## Applying it

• This would work well with Teachit's WW1 resource **Key Stage 3>Poetry>War poetry>Is it right and fitting?** Show first two slides and have students noting their individual response to the question, then show them the Sargent images and combining thoughts and ideas in pairs. Show the slide about mustard gas for the fours discussion, and the final slide for the eights. Then see what they think.

• As a basis for imaginative speech writing, if you (individual, pair, group, class) were elected to run the school, country, or United Nations tomorrow, what policies would you be announcing? Can be linked to citizenship non-fiction themes and articles, or to utopian/dystopian fiction.

• Discuss the role of any main character in any text, with each layer of the discussion pyramid focusing on a different critical moment. Useful for exploring character development and change. With short extracts, can be an interesting pre-teaching activity which really builds predictions and anticipation.

## What's the point?

Research tells us that whatever the group size, without any intervention there is a tendency for two people to hog 60% of the talk-time. If you only ever start with groups of four or five, several students will barely get a look-in, even if they want to. This technique intervenes to encourage everyone to participate. Though it won't necessarily stop the problem as the group sizes increase, at the least it ensures that everyone has contributed at some stage, and at best it breaks the ice at the beginning and may encourage more balanced participation patterns. In addition, the different stages ensure that ideas are well and truly thrashed about. This can be used to value the patient building of collaborative ideas and consensus, as a change from the more competitive individualism of some forms of classroom debate.

## Tricks of the trade

This technique is best suited to questions with wide scope for discussion and a variety of perspectives, and not ones on which students are already likely to have fixed ideas or opinions. The point is genuine discussion. It can get a bit tedious if you have lots of rounds with the same question. A livelier alternative is to vary or develop the question at different stages of the pyramid, and/or introduce additional stimulus material. Students may need some encouragement to pool and explore ideas, rather than just picking the one they think is best in three seconds flat.

## Variations on a theme

• Combine with good questioning techniques to increase the sophistication of the questions with each round, especially where high levels of extension are needed.

• As the groups increase in size encourage less forthcoming students to continue participating by requiring them to present the previous group's thoughts so far. This can also be done randomly – give out coloured cards at the start then round two is someone with a green card, round three a blue card, etc. Don't give your system away, and do the same colour twice sometimes, just to keep 'em guessing.

• For a slow version, introduce additional activities or stimulus materials at each stage and take whatever time is needed for the discussion to reach each mini-conclusion; for a quick version, give each round a time limit and stick to the main question.

# Question cards

To find out what students really want to know

## The basic idea

Each student gets an index card or similar. They write on it a question about the text or topic that they really want to know the answer to. Then they pass their card to the next student. S/he reads it and decides if it's something s/he also wants to know. If yes, the card gets a tick; if no, it doesn't. Students keep passing the cards round until everyone has seen all the questions. Then you use the ticks to guide what happens next: input or activity to find out the answers.

### Applying it

• Use in conjunction with a book jacket as a pre-reading task to stimulate curiosity about the reading that lies ahead.

• Use to prepare questions for a guest speaker or visiting author.

• Use to prepare questions for a hot-seating activity.

### What's the point?

Used at the start of a text or topic, this approach can spark curiosity, help students to think independently about it and explore their own interests and ideas. There is truth in the old adage (or maybe it was something Karl Marx once said…) that if you can articulate the question you are already well on the way to answering it. Used later on in the scheme of work, it can be a valuable tool for checking where students are at in their thinking. It gives immediate feedback about shared problems of understanding, as well as identifying those students who are ready willing and able to take ideas off in more abstract or divergent directions.

### Tricks of the trade

It's all about timing. Allow enough time to make sure students develop questions they really want to know the answers to, not just the first vague question that comes to mind. This will take quiet thinking time. Then in the card-passing phase you need to speed it up and keep it very tight and pacy, otherwise it can get tedious. Encourage divergent thinking, don't stifle it – even questions that initially just seem flippant can lead in interesting directions. And don't necessarily just pick the most popular questions: the most interesting one may well come from the lone ranger.

### Variations on a theme

• Set the questions as research or discussion tasks for different groups or individuals to work on. Their job is to find out the answer and report back.

• Have a whole class Q&A session to see how many of the questions can be answered within the class already, and how many need further input or research.

• If you have a large class and all that card-passing is likely to result in chaos, try doing it standing up in a circle where confusion is minimised and speed can be increased.

### Whizzing it

If you've got a whizzy IWB voting gizmo, type in the questions, get students to vote yes or no to their desire for an answer. Hours of family entertainment there…

# Questioning
## So much more difficult than it looks...

## The basic idea

Ask good questions to encourage students to think in increasingly complex ways. Moving beyond factual recall is much more demanding than it looks. The basic trick is to use more open questions than closed ones, and to ensure that you are never merely inviting the students to guess what is inside your head. Two established taxonomies of questioning can help develop a more sophisticated approach. The idea is to use a variety of questions to encourage higher level thinking.

### Applying it

• Bloom's taxonomy organises the kinds of questions used in classrooms into six types, each increasing in the level of abstraction (see below). Read more in Benjamin S. Bloom, *Taxonomy of Educational Objectives*.

• Socratic questioning takes some practice as its apparent simplicity belies a rigorous approach to questioning that engages students in a challenging dialogue with the teacher. Rather than imposing their own knowledge, the teacher asks questions that will make students think right through their ideas and assertions, to ensure they are accurate, justified and logical. There are seven stages to this process. Once the focus of the dialogue has been determined, specific questions are asked to draw out and develop the students' thinking. The stages are:

1. Choosing a question or topic to work on

2. Students are either given or produce a central statement in response to this question or topic

3. Clarification of the statement e.g. what do you think is the main issue here, or what is your main point?

4. Critical exploration of the assumptions, support, reasons and evidence underpinning the statement, e.g. what are you assuming, what evidence do you have to support that, are these reasons adequate?

5. Exploration of the origin of the statement, e.g. where did you get this idea, have you always felt this way?

6. Examination of the implications and consequences of the statement, e.g. what are you implying by that, what effect would that have?

7. Objective analysis of alternative points of view, e.g. how would other groups of people respond, why have you chosen this perspective rather than that?

• The quick way to do this is to have a fixed number of questions pre-prepared, the slower way is to work through all the levels of thinking, developing each as much as it takes to push the students' thinking along. Done rigorously, Socratic questioning takes a good chunk of time, and it can easily be extended by giving students the opportunity to work up a strong central statement first. More information about Socratic questioning is widely available on the web: just Google it.

### Bloom's Taxonomy

| | |
|---|---|
| **Knowledge** | Observation and recall questions such as who, what, where, when, as well as those involving listing and labelling things, defining or describing them. |
| **Comprehension** | Interpretation questions requiring summary, contrast, prediction, estimation, discussion and differentiation. |
| **Application** | Questions that necessitate the use of information to solve, prove and show, and to classify, experiment and change. |
| **Analysis** | Questions that interrogate components and meanings, requiring selection, comparison, inference and explanation. |
| **Synthesis** | Questions that link ideas together to create new ones through combination, modification, design, invention, creation and speculation. |
| **Evaluation** | Questions that interrogate the value and validity of ideas, by assessing, ranking, testing, making recommendations, justifying and convincing. |

## What's the point?

It is very easy to ask questions - especially when you are tired and under pressure to cover a lot of content - that are little more than interludes in a didactic presentation. The student's task is not to provide interesting or original insights, even to think very much at all, but simply to guess the correct response so that the teacher can move on. When this kind of questioning happens, students who give unanticipated answers can very quickly get labelled as disruptive. This is a waste of potentially rich and interesting lines of classroom enquiry, and shuts down the feedback you get about what understanding students have of the topic. Good questioning opens the mind's doors, helping to develop critical enquiry and intellectual curiosity.

## Tricks of the trade

Don't rush to answer the question you have asked if there is silence. Research suggests that the longest pause we allow before rephrasing or filling the silence is just two seconds. Practise extending this by counting slowly to five or ten or twenty. It feels like a game of chicken at first, but if you can do it without fidgeting or pacing up and down nervously, eventually someone will start the discussion off, if only to ask a question of clarification.

## Variations on a theme

• Get students asking you 20 questions about a new topic, to identify what they already know and what they want to know.

• For Advanced Literature students Teachit's resource **Key Stage 4/5>Skills>A/AS Essentials>Whose theme is it anyway?** uses higher order questions to explore themes and to consider what discussion can contribute to the development of ideas.

• In whole class discussion, you might sometimes choose to ask different students different types of questions to differentiate. Just be aware that thinking skills are developed by thinking, and if no-one ever asks a student to do the hard stuff s/he is unlikely to make much progress.

• For a creative extension of this kind of activity, students could look at question and answer feature articles such as 'Passnotes' in the *Guardian*.

## Whizzing it

Set up an online discussion forum on your school/college intranet, or using a shared blog. Establish a topic, start off with a lower order question and drip-feed higher order ones as the discussion gets going. Even better, teach students how to use one of the taxonomies of questioning and practise it in class a number of times until everyone has got the general hang of it. Then get them to take turns being the questioner in your online discussion forum.

# Quick on the draw

Parlour game fun with tricky texts

## The basic idea

Lots of plain paper, some pens, pencils, crayons or whatever will best encourage artistic licence, and a text students are struggling to understand by virtue of its language complexity or stylistic challenge. Divide the text into meaningful sense units. Read each one aloud. Pause. Students have to draw whatever it is they 'see' when they hear these words. Repeat the sense unit two or three times if needed. Afterwards, get students to compare what they drew, refer back to the text, reread, consider, and decide what meanings and interpretations can be derived.

### Applying it

- Explore ideas about how meaning is encoded in language. Teachit's resource **Key Stage 3>Poetry> Beowulf and Jabberwocky> 'Jabberwocky'** could be extended with this activity before writing definitions of the invented words.

- Use to explore powerful speeches or soliloquies where you want students to get on the inside of the language. Try Lady Macbeth's 'Come, you spirits' or Macbeth's 'Tomorrow, and tomorrow, and tomorrow'.

- Use to help students explore the power of imagery in poetry: try it with Blake's 'London' or Keats' 'To Autumn' and see what happens.

- Also works at AS level: much to my surprise, my class claimed not to understand a word of John Donne's 'Elegy On His Mistress Going To Bed'. Worked a treat and made me cry laughing but the resulting images did have to go in the shredder!

### What's the point?

This activity can really help students to unfreeze their brains by coming at the problem from a completely different direction. It can help visual learners find ways into a text and encourages creativity and openness of response. It teaches students to deal with problems by breaking them down into manageable chunks. You can also see immediately and precisely which parts of the text are causing the most problem, so that you can target the help needed. And it can be great fun.

### Tricks of the trade

Prepare for the activity by explaining the point carefully, making sure everyone understands that this is free thinking time and responses will be evaluated afterwards. Tell them anything goes as long as it is an honest response to the words they hear, and get them to draw individually. Keep it snappy and immediate. Don't give students too long to think about it or brains will start switching back into anxious judgement mode. There is only any point doing this activity with texts that are really challenging.

### Variations on a theme

- For revision of the GCSE AQA A poetry anthology try Teachit's fun picture game **Key Stage 4>Poetry>Poems from Different Cultures>Different Cultures Cluster 1 – picture quiz**. Similarly try Teachit's **Key Stage 4>Prose>Of Mice and Men by John Steinbeck>Chapters 3 and 4 – Picture quiz**.

### Whizzing it

Use the ideas generated from the quick-fire drawing stage to develop animated multi-media versions of the text that highlight and develop key ideas of meaning and interpretation.

# Quiz

The obvious plus student DIY

## The basic idea

Test student knowledge and understanding, either individually or collectively, but definitely at the fun end of the testing spectrum. Use a simple list of questions, divide it into pub-quiz style themed rounds, or go the whole hog and do it in the style of your favourite TV quiz show.

### Applying it

• Try using the *Who Wants To Be A Millionaire?* format with Teachit's **Key Stage 3>Prose>Oliver Twist (NLS Y8) by Charles Dickens>Who Wants To Be A Dickensiannaire?**

• For a lively variety of questions that could be used in rounds, check out Teachit's Seamus Heaney quiz **Key Stage 4>GCSE>Seamus Heaney - GCSE>How well do you know Seamus Heaney?**

• For a more challenging approach try Teachit's **Key Stage 3/4>Drama> Macbeth>Think of Three** in which all the answers are trios.

### What's the point?

A quiz can bring a bit of healthy competition into the classroom. As with anything, it's not what you do it's the way that you do it. Learning how to lose graciously is also a valuable social skill in a culture that values losing so highly! It can also give some light relief after a period of intense study, as well as providing useful feedback to you and your students about the parts of the course that few reached.

### Tricks of the trade

To save yourself work, use ready-made quizzes, specifically from Teachit or more generally on the web. The biggest trick to this, however, is to think through how you are going to keep the excitement and noise under control. Have everyone shouting answers out at the same time and you'll end up with a headache and not a lot of meaningful learning. Any format where individual answers or secretive whispering are required is good! Projecting the questions onto the big screen means you don't have to repeat them 36 times. Make sure you have enough variation in the format to sustain student interest. Picture rounds, clips rounds, matching tasks – whatever your imagination can dream up, but keep it lively and keep it moving along at a pace, and give the answers at the end of each round to

hype up the drama and avoid death-by-too-many-answers at the end. Prizes? In my classroom the glory is everything. And finally, always let groups pick their team name. Always…

### Variations on a theme

• Have a joker to play in one round of the team's choice, for which all points scored are doubled – gets them thinking about their strengths and weaknesses.

• Have questions with different point values and make them choose which point value to play.

• Get students to write quizzes for each other and you've immediately planned two lessons for the price of one. Excellent learning takes place as each group attempts to write the most perfectly fiendish question. Pick the best questions from each, combine them, and you've also got a useful revision resource.

• To slow it down have multiple rounds; to speed it up do a short set of multiple choice questions with a prize for the fastest set of correct answers.

• If you're asking individuals questions, prepare differentiated questions so you can set an appropriate level of individual challenge.

• Try challenging other local schools or colleges. Alternatively, invite undergraduates or PGCE students to host a mega-quiz session.

### Whizzing it

If you've got the kit, use those interactive whiteboard voting gizmo things. Or use quiz writing software, such as 'Hot Potatoes', and get students to do your quiz online for homework. There are lots of free quiz writing tools on the internet that enable you to email the quiz to students and their scores are sent back to you automatically while you doze peacefully in front of the telly.

# Quote quest

## That hoary old chestnut

## The basic idea

There are two basic versions. In the first, students are charged with the task of finding and selecting the best quotes to illustrate a particular view of a character, a theme, a line of argument, a setting or mood, etc. Alternatively, in the reverse quote quest students are given a pile of quotes to sort through and organise into key ideas, explain the significance of, find who said them, or select the most important from.

### Applying it

- For a nice simple who said what in *Twelfth Night* quote quest, try Teachit's **Key Stage 3/4>Drama>Twelfth Night – Act 3 Scene 4>Work book 3**.

- To develop this approach, add a 'why?' and a 'when' to the 'who said it?' as in Teachit's **Key Stage 4>Drama>An Inspector Calls by J.B. Priestley>Quote quest: Who said it? When? Why?** and likewise for *Measure for Measure* in the Key Stage 5 Drama library.

- For an example of a quote quest that builds into a good revision game try Teachit's **Key Stage 4/5>Poetry>Advanced poetry essentials>Quote quest and 'On The Spot' game**. Originally designed for work on Marvell but would work for any poet.

### What's the point?

To encourage close attention to specific textual evidence and/or to practise the selection of short apt quotation. Being able to select judiciously a small part from a large whole is a demanding skill. In the selection process students often fine tune their interpretation in the light of new or contradictory evidence. If different selections are compared, good work can be done to encourage the justification of choices.

### Tricks of the trade

It can get a bit boring if done in isolation. It is much more interesting if linked to activities that involve applying the quotations to some meaningful purpose, such as preparation for hot-seating, writing a feature article, a debate, etc.

### Variations on a theme

- For extension, get students to compare and contrast quotes from the text with quotes selected from another work by the same writer, or other writers, or a secondary source.

- To provide different levels of challenge, require different numbers or lengths of quotes to be selected – fewer/shorter can be much tougher as tighter selection criteria have to be applied. A free selection is harder than selection from a given range.

- In tortoise mode, work on selection to support a range of ideas, encourage comparative discussion and link in to an application task; in hare mode, use for closure or revision, inviting the selection of 10, 15 or 20 most useful multi-purpose quotations.

### Whizzing it

Copy a scene or chapter or set of poems into Word. Get students to select the most important quotations, highlight them and create pop-up boxes giving explanations of their significance. They could annotate their whole e-text like this!

# Ranking

Simple, diamond, triangles and bullseyes

## The basic idea

Students sort a series of ideas into rank order of importance. They can first determine the ideas themselves, or these can be given, or they can be given with scope for tweaking and adaptation. Listing and/or numbering ideas in rank order is the simplest format, but there are others, as below.

**Applying it**

- As a pre-reading task, try ranking the qualities of a good partner in Teachit's *Key Stage 3>Drama>Much Ado About Nothing>What makes a good partner?*

- Add a ranking activity to the Teachit resource *Key Stage 3>Prose> Brother in the Land by Robert Swindells>The survival game – objects*, after students have selected eight items they would hope to have following a nuclear war.

- Have students selecting the nine most important quotations which represent Lady Macbeth's character, then diamond ranking them.

- Analyse the logical structure of famous speeches (real or movie) using the pyramid ranking diagram to identify the key proposition, supporting ideas, examples and details, rhetorical devices, etc. Lots of resources to support this at **www.americanrhetoric.com**.

- Use the bulls eye ranking to explore layers of detail about themes in *Measure for Measure*, e.g. appearance, love, justice, and self-knowledge. Detailed notes on these are available in Teachit's *Key Stage 5>Drama>Measure for Measure>Themes in the play*. Have groups working on one theme each, or each group doing all four.

*(continued over)*

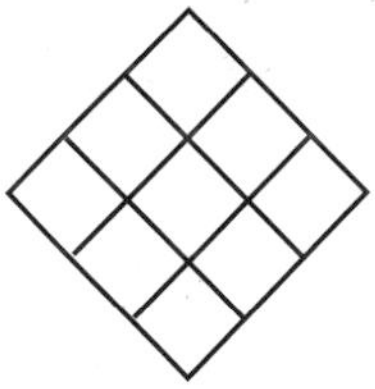

|---|---|
| | **Diamond ranking**<br><br>Take nine ideas. Students put the single most important at the top of the diamond; then the next two most important underneath; then the next three; then two; then the least important at the bottom of the diamond. Can also be done with bigger diamonds but gets a bit unwieldy. |
| 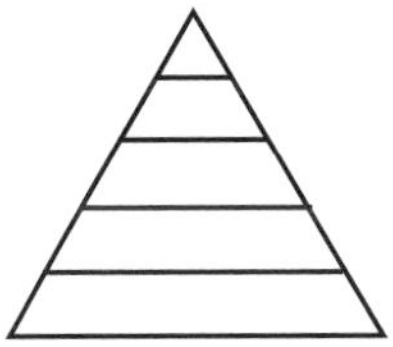 | **Pyramid ranking** (though it looks like a triangle to me...)<br><br>Take x ideas. Students put the most important idea at the top and work their way down. This can also be used to build layers of detail in imaginative writing, or layers of a paragraph to develop writing skills. |
| 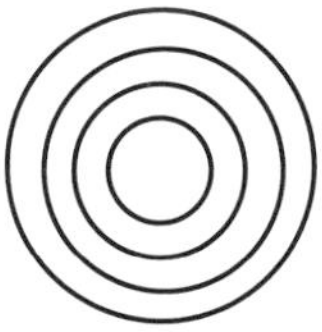 | **Bulls eye ranking**<br><br>The big idea goes in the centre, with subsidiary ideas building outwards as before. Try dividing the diagram into three or four segments, and get the students mapping their ideas about different themes. |

R

## What's the point?

It encourages careful selection and prioritisation of information. This generates much debate, as different perspectives, attitudes and values amongst the students are explored. Visualising complex written texts as layers of different types of detail can help students to 'see' the task of writing as something a bit more challenging than whacking the first basic idea down on the page. It can also help in developing the ability to discriminate, in reading complex texts, between different types of information.

## Tricks of the trade

Diamond ranking works especially well if you have the ideas available on cards (or blank ones they can write the ideas onto) that can be moved around. This encourages playfulness with ideas as different options can easily be tried and tested. It is usually more motivating for students if they get to choose the ideas in the first place, or at least get to modify them – after all, you might not have picked the best or most interesting ones.

Create A3 ranking diagrams, whack them through the laminator and you have a wipe-clean resource ready for group work.

## Variations on a theme

- The old survival scenario ranking activity has a well worn pedigree. See **www.wilderdom.com>***Index to Group Activities & Games>Most popular games>Survival Scenarios* for lots of useful resources. Very good for exploring team decision making dynamics, and leads in nicely to work on *Robinson Crusoe*, *Desert Island Discs*, and imaginative storytelling on survival themes.

- Mix it up by giving different students different sets of ideas to work with, or different size ranking grids e.g. a nine item diamond or a 13 item diamond.

## Whizzing it

Use the many IWB ranking exercises available on Teachit, such as:

*Key Stage 3>Drama>Macbeth>Leadership and ranking activity [IWB]* – characters are ranked according to their power at three key points in the play.

*Key Stage 3/4>Prose>Stone Cold by Robert Swindells>Perceptions of the homeless* – rank common views of homeless people from positive to negative.

*Key Stage 4/5>Drama>Othello> Judging Othello* – rank Othello's actions from least to most awful.

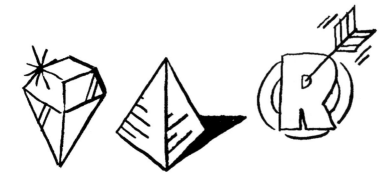

# Reading comprehension

How to make it less boring

## The basic idea

Reading comprehension is one of those things we all do without even thinking too much about it, because it is likely to have been a major part of our education in any subject dealing with written texts. But in case you somehow managed to miss it, you give students a text and ask them a set of questions about it, which they have to answer in writing, usually with the rubric 'You must give your answers in complete sentences'. Why? What's that about? Who ever does that ever again in their life?!

### Applying it

• Allow students to make bullet point notes. In Teachit's resource *Key Stage 3>Poetry>Canterbury Tales> Canterbury Tales Resource pack (2 – while reading)*, students complete a form with notes about the Miller's clothes and props, as well as space for student descriptions and responses. This also mixes things up with some listening comprehension from an online audio file.

• Mix up the types of questions, to include straightforward comprehension questions, mini-diagrams, and personal response, as in this Teachit resource *Key Stage 3>Prose> Mystery – The Monkey's Paw> Comprehension questions and activities*.

• Mix it up some more with word lists and opportunities to draw sketches as in Teachit's *Key Stage 3/4>Poetry> War poetry> 'The Charge of the Light Brigade' activity pack*.

• Try giving students a summary or explanation of the text in which several factual mistakes have been made. The task is to spot them and correct them.

• A cheap tactic if you have closed answers is to make them part of an anagram or an acrostic or a crossword. Well, it livens up the preparation anyway…

*(continued over)*

## What's the point?

Reading comprehension can be a useful activity, in focusing student attention on key aspects of a text that they might otherwise miss, in finding and exploring relevant details for application in some other task, in getting them mining the text for its treasure.

## Tricks of the trade

Let's face it, though, reading comprehension can also be one of the dreariest tasks known to humanity, little better than copying wadges of the text out. That's asking for trouble unless you have a class full of robots. Creating a more positive experience is partly a matter of asking more interesting questions (see **Questioning** on page 106, for more on this), partly good differentiation so that not everyone has to churn out stuff they could spot from three miles away, and partly about mini-tactics that just mix it up a bit. Don't just rely on the mini-tactics listed above: focus on all three aspects and use sparingly as a technique. And don't set reading comprehension homework. Ever. It's far too boring and you'll only end up chasing it for weeks until you wish you'd never bothered.

## Variations on a theme

• Get the students setting the questions for each other or for you, instead of the other way round. Much more interesting, especially if you get students into the swing of writing more fun, interactive questions.

• Or try this variation: a student reads a text or extract and turns it into a combination of pictures, symbols and words, but using as few words as possible. Then the text or extract is given to a second student and the first student relates the information to them, using their pictures as support and with the second student checking the accuracy and detail of their comprehension. And the twist in the tale? The second student then has to report back the information to the rest of the class without the text or the images.

• Also try reading comprehension through information gap activities. Give students different versions of the information or text you want them to explore, and a set of questions that focus on facts, opinions or ideas drawn from both. Two different versions will create pairs who need to collaborate to help each other fill the gaps in their knowledge; three will produce trios; four will produce quads; any more than that produces Bedlam. Try it with different extracts of reviews or book jacket blurbs, or with different clues from a mystery story.

## Whizzing it

Use Teachit's interactive comprehension resources, such as **Key Stage 3/4>Drama>Macbeth>Dynamic activities.** Once students are used to this kind of thing, get them creating their own for other texts…

# Readings

By teachers, students, writers and performers

## The basic idea

Reading aloud is good...

### Applying it

• Poetry is, at its roots, an oral form, and the aural texture matters in understanding it. Students can only develop that richness of understanding if they feel poetry in their mouths, and are immersed in good readings of it. Always read poems to your class or use recordings; frequently get them to read them to each other; take every opportunity to bring poets into your classroom, live or recorded.

• Novelists are always reading their work to audiences. Look out for local sightings.

• Simon Callow received critical acclaim for dressing up as Charles Dickens and giving readings from his work. Now there's an idea ripe for adaptation...

• Working on speeches? Get students feeling the power of oratory as a physical thing, not just an exercise in persuasive argument. Get the hall booked for a lesson and see what it takes to make Martin Luther King's words grab people's attention at the back of the room, never mind at the back of a major demonstration.

### What's the point?

It gets students inside the language of the text, exploring how sound works with meaning, how tone affects interpretation, and how literature is far more than the sum of its technical components. Powerful oral expression is not just about what is said but also how it is said, and practising that physical act is as important as redrafting the words. Often unexpected talents emerge – give them an opportunity to thrive. It can also be very powerful in liberating meaning if students are struggling to read a pre-20th century text – audio books are a great resource and are starting to become available in mp3 format (try **www.audible.co.uk**) as well as on CD-ROM. Read aloud by someone who understands the rhythm of the lines or sentences, it magically comes alive.

### Tricks of the trade

Practise your own readings first, especially if it's a long text. I like to give myself a reading script if it's something new, enlarged and annotated with scribbles to mark my pauses, slow bits and fast bits, emphases, tone etc. When working on student readings, encourage creative experimentation, perhaps giving them two or three tones or styles to try a passage or poem in as a stimulus to them discussing and deciding what works best. As with oral work, especially on booming great speeches, make sure the class next door isn't taking a test! Well, not unless you want another teacher to set fire to your pigeonhole/car/hair.

### Variations on a theme

• This kind of work is a good opportunity to talk about punctuation in a meaningful way, exploring what values different marks have in informing our reading of the lines or sentences.

• Get a writer in residence who will do some workshops, do some writing about being in school or on a theme worked on with students too, and finish with a grand finale of readings. Skint? See if your local university has a creative writing programme and blag a student or lecturer to do something cool as part of their schools liaison/widening participation work.

### Whizzing it

Get students recording themselves reading passages or poems, rerecording until they're happy with it, and then whack them on the intranet for sharing and comparing – with each other, with recorded luvvies, etc. Alternatively get them making their own *Poetry Please* (BBC Radio 4) magazine programme of readings and podcast to the nation.

# Right to reply
## The underdog speaks

## The basic idea

Take one or more of the characters who can't get a word in edgeways in a scene or situation. Let them have their say! It's that simple…

### Applying it.

- Carol Ann Duffy's *The World's Wife* has 30 women from myth and history telling their stories. Take any one poem and see what else students can come up with in their own creative writing.

- Margaret Atwood does it brilliantly in *Good Bones* with Gertrude's reply to Hamlet in the 'rank sweat of an enseamed bed' scene (Act III Scene 4). Probably about time Ophelia had her right to reply too.

- Works a treat with those great 17th century argumentative poems, Andrew Marvell's 'To His Coy Mistress' and to John Donne's 'Elegy on his Mistress Going to Bed' and 'The Flea'. Use to explore ideas about gender in a fun way.

### What's the point?

Students have to read closely and imaginatively between the lines to develop a reply. It invites good discussion of the power dynamics of the scene or situation, and close attention to the way a character speaks or doesn't speak contributes to their characterisation. Exploring why a character doesn't speak can help develop students' understanding of how language works in society, and giving a voice to the powerless is obviously a good thing. Empathetic work like this is good for any student's soul and will give those with high emotional intelligence an opportunity to thrive.

### Tricks of the trade

The key trick is to choose good scenes or situations that will appeal strongly to

your class. Those described above tend to appeal more strongly to female students. This isn't a reason not to do it with boys, but it's probably helpful to contextualise the task as a way in to understanding the significant gender dynamics of the text, period, and canonical literature. If it's likely to cause a problem, don't do it! The other trick, if your head of department starts twitching about league tables, is to bring the discussion back to the original text afterwards in order to draw together what has been learned about it.

### Variations on a theme

- It can be done as written work and/or spoken performance. If written, an extra challenge can be provided, as appropriate, by encouraging students to write it in the same form as the original. The wall display of very funny Donne's women poems made at least one Ofsted inspector swoon with joy…

- Once students have developed their reply, get them experimenting with **Intercutting** (see page 59) of the original and the creation to see what creative things start happening.

- Can include or lead in to very nice research into social and historical context.

### Whizzing it

Lots of opportunities here for creative multimedia texts. Simple illustrated documents putting the two texts in parallel… make your font-fiddlers happy with intercut texts that use fonts to show the different speakers… get the whiz-kids doing intercut audio ordings… animated texts…

# Role play & simulation

Walking a mile in someone else's shoes

## The basic idea

Each student assumes a role in a particular scenario. In role, they interact with each other to resolve a conflict, make a decision, solve a problem, or complete a task. In so doing they explore possible ways of behaving in a situation they could conceivably encounter, and ways of talking and responding to others. Simulation is kind of like role play except that the situation is bigger and more engaging. To get that effect it usually relies on a greater level of real world connection, very powerful and emotive themes and issues, and decisions that seriously affect people's lives. The roles are well defined and students work through a series of activities designed to prompt key decision making processes. These simulation 'games' get students on the inside of an issue and can lead to superb persuasive and empathetic writing.

### Applying it

• Try Teachit's role play of a gossip magazine editorial meeting at *Key Stage 3/4>Skills>Speaking and listening tasks>Magazine role play*, or of a school council meeting to decide how to spend a sum of money at *Key Stage 3/4>Skills>Speaking and listening tasks>Spend some of the school's money!*

• Take any political hot potato and get students playing roles in a TV current affairs interview programme, with a politician and an interviewer. The task of the interviewer is to uncover a truth the politician doesn't want to reveal.

• Another popular and successful activity involves students being the various interested parties at a meeting to decide the fate of a planning application in the locality. Lots of scope to explore and explode stereotypical attitudes – Outraged of Tunbridge Wells, Corporate Bad Guy, Wet Liberal *Guardian* Reader, Mr and Mrs NIMBY, etc.

• Christian Aid has some excellent simulation resources, such as the Trading Trainers game which is available as a free download from **www.christianaid.org.uk >le@rn zone>schools>Simulation games**. Oxfam produce similar materials.

*(continued over)*

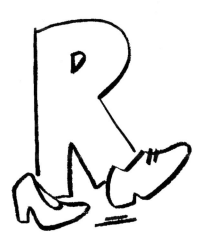

## What's the point?

It gets students engaged with a scenario without them needing to act, which can be a blessing for the dramatically challenged. It still manages to encourage empathy and imagination, and provides an opportunity to practise oral skills in lifelike situations. To get to a decision, some kind of negotiation or conflict resolution is usually required, and practising that is a good enough end in itself. Playing a simulation game requires complex collaboration and co-operation with other people, and a whole range of real world oral skills in order to 'survive' or get things done. Most educational simulations are designed to take about an hour and a half and, facilitated well, students often get swept up into another world losing all sense of time and self. That is a valuable experience that won't be forgotten in a hurry.

## Tricks of the trade

Get as many students involved as possible. Watching two people do it at the front of the classroom (unless they've volunteered after everyone's already had a go) is more often than not a boring waste of time and space for the rest of the class. Apart from that, try and limit your role to observation as much as possible. Let students try out different ways of responding. And always – absolutely always - debrief them afterwards with the key question: how did it feel to be in this role? This brings everyone back to reality, and is especially important if someone has been role-playing someone unpleasant.

## Variations on a theme

• Have everyone in role all role-playing simultaneously in small groups; even better, attach an observer to each small group whose task will be to feedback thoughtful observations about what happened afterwards.

• Try doing the old 'May I?' technique. Two people (or however many the situation warrants…) role play in the middle of a circle of students. If another student feels s/he could be doing a better job, then s/he taps the role player on the shoulder. That person can give way or not as s/he sees fit.

• Give students an opportunity to role play the situation to a single resolution; or get them to try doing it using two or three distinctly different approaches; or get them to do it once, evaluate how it could be improved and then re-do.

• Chat up your local branch of Christian Aid or Oxfam, or any other charity you think might be useful, and get them to come and run the simulation for you! Or your local university branch of the same…

• If the simulation you do receives cries of 'That's pants sir/miss!' get them rewriting it and testing it out with younger pupils. Writing a simulation is an interesting narrative art.

## Whizzing it

Let students loose on computer simulation games, such as running a theme park, or building a civilisation. Once you can tear them away again, get them writing fantastical 'Rise and Fall of a Great Empire' stories or creating their own games.

# Round robin

Discussion technique to get everyone involved

## The basic idea

Kind of like a blown-up game of consequences. Give groups of students a problem, a question, a text, etc. They discuss it, or any part of it that they find fruitful, for a given amount of time. At the end of this they provide a summary of their ideas on a flipchart, which then gets passed round to the next group. They follow up ideas, interrogate assumptions, add examples, explore additional parts of the text, speculate, etc and add their ideas to the flipchart accordingly. It keeps going like this until each group gets its original sheet back, by now covered in ideas. They draw all this thinking together and formulate a coherent solution to the problem, answer to the question, or interpretation of the text.

### Applying it

- Give each group one poem by the set poet or thematically connected poems from a set anthology and finish with group presentations on each.

- Give groups key speeches or sections of dialogue from the play which collectively show character change. End with 'this moment' presentations that lead into whole class discussion of change.

- Give each group a different stanza of a poem as their starting point, display the flipcharts for everyone to view, and finish with whole class discussion of the complete poem.

### What's the point?

It encourages collaborative and creative generation and development of ideas rather than modelling the unrealistic and lonely practice of the individual awaiting a moment of divine inspiration. It is dynamic and can be moderately frustrating, in a good way, in that students just start getting into an idea when you move them on. Handled well, that builds them to a bigger climax, in a manner of speaking…

### Tricks of the trade

Timing is everything of course. You need to listen attentively, and move it on at precisely that moment at which the volume dips to a low buzz. Insist on swift and simultaneous circulation of papers so that groupwork doesn't get out of synch.

### Variations on a theme

- To mix it up, give different groups different responsibilities e.g. one group must focus on the most powerful words, one striking images and patterns of imagery, one on the structure, one on line and metre, one on rhyme and aural effects, etc. Select groups on the basis of their ability to handle these responsibilities.

- To speed it up have a more narrowly focused task and short rounds; to slow it down have a more open task and longer rounds.

- Use a target diagram to keep track of which ideas were added in which round.

# Slide show

As exploration of the cultural context of the text (mainly for AS/A2?..)

## The basic idea

Take some works of art (well, okay, maybe just some decent reproductions…) that draw on similar cultural and philosophical contexts as your literary text. As a pre-reading exercise, students explore the art works, identifying themes and patterns, connections and attitudes, and what they find interesting. Link these ideas and perspectives to the text as you read and watch bigger ideas build.

### Applying it

• Pre-Raphaelite paintings often strike a chord with young people and link well to the study of Shakespeare, Tennyson and Keats.

• Romantic paintings work well for helping students see the significance of the settings in Frankenstein.

• Victorian prints of workhouses, orphanages and factories are good for many a Dickens novel.

• Works well with Modernist art and Eliot's *The Wasteland*, as students start to understand the style as a verbal equivalent of the visual.

### What's the point?

Imaginative engagement with the cultural milieu of the text, without the students needing to have any prior knowledge or experience of it. All they have to do is say what they see, and you help them build ideas and connections into an understanding of key themes and stylistic issues. The sense of excitement that comes from discovering connections between works of art (and between school/college subjects) can be tangible, especially for strong students and/or those interested in Art. Images work well in generating lively discussion.

### Tricks of the trade

With digital images and a data projector (or the trendy retro-tech of slides and a slide projector), this is a pleasant opportunity to turn all the lights off and not have to look at 'em for half an hour… But if your students riot under cover of darkness, nice big laminated prints work just as well. The real trick is careful selection of images, partly to bring out useful points for the reading of the text, partly to intrigue and puzzle your students into thinking beyond the surface 'It's a picture of a horse.'

### Variations on a theme

• Give students the opportunity to research for themselves the cultural context and select images to illustrate its key thematic and stylistic concerns.

• Speed it up with a small number of tightly focused images and directed questions; slow it down with lots of images and open discussion. Move on to quotations or short extracts from the text which highlight thematic and stylistic issues identified.

• An alternative to the 'say what you see' activity is to let each student choose a different image. They write a short story based on it. Then get them listening to each other's stories to identify patterns and connections.

### Whizzing it

Need some images? Check out Tate Online at **www.tate.org.uk** for 65,000. Should keep your class busy for a few minutes, anyway. Drop images into Word and use all the gadgets and gizmos on your IWB to annotate them with comments.

# Spot the difference

Oh, for the lost puzzle books of one's youth...

## The basic idea

Give the students two or more texts and get them to identify as many differences as they can. Leave this as a completely open question and see what they find, or set a predetermined number of items to find, and/or a predetermined range. The texts could consist of one base and one or more modified versions, or they could be different bases to start with.

### Applying it

• Give students a draft and final version of a text and get them to spot the differences first before moving in to discussion of the effects of those differences. A classic version of this activity uses the final version and one of the many early drafts of Wilfred Owen's 'Anthem for Doomed Youth'.

• Accuracy work on spelling, grammar and punctuation. Two versions of a text: spot the differences and then identify which version is correct.

• Give students two images of different productions of a play and invite them to spot general or specific differences.

• Also works well with different posters for the same film: use the Internet Movie Database **www.imdb.com** for as many examples as you could ever need.

### What's the point?

It can be used to encourage close scrutiny of a text or image, paying attention to small details, and to build the ability to make fine discriminations between things. This can help to develop accuracy, or an understanding of subtle choices made by writers. When the question is left open, it allows students creative space to generate new ideas, and to see things in their own way. Good things often come of that.

### Tricks of the trade

Pick good texts or images to work with, ones which will appeal to your students and make them want to bother paying close attention. If you can build in some kind of puzzle or mystery to solve while they're at it, you're on to a winner.

### Variations on a theme

• Select three images of a story, such as the slaying by St George of the Dragon. Students spot as many differences as they can, then discuss which bits they like best in each. Move into creative writing and/or exploration of Fanthorpe's poem based on Uccello's painting. Search for 'dragon' on the National Gallery's website for four such images **www.nationalgallery.org.uk**.

### Whizzing it

Get images or texts up side by side on the big screen and use the IWB to annotate with observed differences.

# Stage directions

Exit, pursued by a bear

## The basic idea

Take a play which has very few stage directions. Anything by that Shakespeare geezer works well for this. Students take a scene or section and add as many stage directions as they like to show how they think the scene should be performed.

### Applying it

- Watch a scene from a film version of the play and write the stage directions that the director has embodied in the film. Seeing someone else's choices in action first can really help students get the hang of it before they start producing their own.

- Use it as an induction activity with different students working on a variety of scenes or speeches from a play by Shakespeare.

- Take a play that has both stage directions and an e-text form. Delete the stage directions and get students writing their own. Compare with the writer's version.

### What's the point?

It makes students visualise the scene, with movements, gestures, props, tone of voice etc all being brought to mind, but without needing any expert practical knowledge of staging or performance.

Good for teachers/students who loathe acting it out in class. Brings the text to life, as well as making interpretations of the scene tangible. Worked on in groups it makes for lively discussion and exploration of alternative ways of seeing the text. It provides an active basis for comparison with film/TV/stage productions.

### Tricks of the trade

Give students some help in identifying the kinds of information that might be useful in a stage direction, and what stage directions are for. Perhaps show them some extreme examples. Definitely give them an adapted copy of the scene or section with spaces to write in, rather than expecting them to squidge it all between the lines in a book.

### Variations on a theme

- Let students do it visually as well as or instead of in written form. Sketches, diagrams, colours, whatever makes clear their realisation of the scene.

- Set the extra challenge either before or after they've done the main task, perhaps for those who finish quickly, of only being allowed to keep a certain number of directions. Which will they cut, which will they keep?

- For a quick lesson, limit the number of directions from the start and get students working in groups. To extend, start with individual writing then move into group work to decide and develop which ones are most useful. Students could swap the newly created texts and have a go at acting each other's version of the scene out before discussing the differences between their interpretations.

### Whizzing it

Give students the text in electronic format and let them type in their stage directions where they want them to go, using different fonts to their heart's content.

# Still life

Photos and screen captures from productions and telly

## The basic idea

Get students discussing stills: acquired from education resource packs, illustrated texts, or through a data capture card. Go further and get students to justify the selection of one or more that they think best captures the essence of a character, an event or a setting; best shows the way something about the text changes; or illuminates the differences of interpretation in different productions. Instant stimulation of top drawer discussion.

### Applying it

• For film stills check out the stonking Internet Movie Database at **www.imdb.com**. Search for the film then look for the links on the left to **Photo gallery** and/or **>Photographs**. Loads of good stills from Baz Luhrmann's *Romeo + Juliet* there, and several of Marlon Brando with his shirt off in Elia Kazan's *A Streetcar Named Desire*.

• Google 'production photos' and the name of the play you are working on and see what you get. Loads of amateur production photos for Timberlake Wertenbaker's *Our Country's Good*…

• At least two publishers have produced CD-ROMs of some Shakespeare texts with loads of production stills. Not a cheap option so try before you buy. Check out Longman School Shakespeare's Teacher's CD-ROMs and Cambridge School Shakespeare picture collection CD-ROMS.

### What's the point?

Visual images are a rich resource that allow a closeness of focus on specific moments or issues of representation. Details can be seen that may get lost when watching the film, TV or stage

production, and the presence of a tangible resource can give less confident students a useful starting point for discussion. Selecting a small number of images from many encourages students to justify their choices, engage in shared decision making and commit to an interpretation. There are also great opportunities for comparative discussion – er, and for nice classroom displays.

### Tricks of the trade

Use this technique with a text where there are many possibilities for selection and differences in choices will spark interesting discussion. You don't want to set this up where there is one obvious clear-runner of an answer that they will all choose.

### Variations on a theme

• Use short clips instead of images if you have sufficient access to multimedia resources.

• In the short version students look at a given set of images, make their selection and justify it to the rest of the class. In longer versions, students might create their own sets of images, spend more time in comparative discussion, and follow up with written analysis or creative transformation into a production poster or educational wallchart.

• Laminate the images, give students non-permanent OHP pens (there has to be some remaining use for this retro-technology) and then they can scribble their notes and ideas (and moustaches) all over them. Ideal for the inveterate fiddlers in your class.

### Whizzing it

With digital images available, get students using ICT to prepare PowerPoint presentations, production posters or educational wallcharts.

# Storyboard
## Seeing narrative sequences

## The basic idea

A storyboard is a filmmaker's tool for visualising a narrative, a kind of visual script. It uses a sequence of sketches, as in a cartoon strip, to show what the viewer will see and the kinds of camera shot used. It may also have notes detailing the kind of setting and what the viewer will hear, in terms of dialogue and sound track. So, you get students producing their visual scripts of a scene or chapter or poem, or an advertisement or trailer of their own creation. Useful examples available here **www.thestoryboardartist.com**.

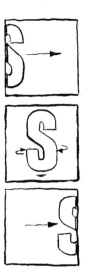

## Applying it

- For a basic template see Teachit's *Key Stage 3/4>Media & Non-Fiction>Media and non-fiction basics>Blank storyboard sheet*.

- For a more advanced media template see the second page of Teachit's *Key Stage 4/5>Media & Non-Fiction Film>Creating a film noir*.

- Check out Teachit's must-have resource amendments with Lego people illustrating the different camera shot types *Key Stage 3/4>Media & Non-Fiction>Media and non-fiction basics>Useful generic blank storyboard*.

- Get students producing the storyboard for a TV advert for a particular product. Chocolate is perennially popular but for variation (and more challenge) try getting them to market it to a less obvious age group than their own.

- Take some of the poems from your anthology and get groups producing storyboards for a dramatised presentation of them for a 'The Nation's Most Loathed Poems' programme. Or something like that anyway...

- Great for highlighting key events in long narrative poems: specify a set number of frames for storyboarding Tennyson's 'The Lady of Shalott', Coleridge's 'The Rime of the Ancient Mariner', or Keats' 'Isabella, or The Pot of Basil'.

- At AS/A2, set them the task of storyboarding the eyeball gouging scene in *King Lear*, and then discuss the critical opinion that this scene is unstageable.

## What's the point?

It's a highly creative task, requiring imaginative realisation of the words on the page, the ability to think simultaneously in the different dimensions of sound and vision, and an understanding of how narrative tension and pace work in a different medium. Very challenging, and yet students often leap at the chance to do this kind of thing because they feel more comfortable and confident with the language of film.

## Tricks of the trade

Give students examples to look at if they have not come across this technique before as it can take ages to explain clearly what you mean. Have lots of copies of templates available, or the means by which more can be printed off, as this is an activity in which creativity is to be strongly encouraged. And creativity always involves lots of screwed up bits of paper in the bin. If you can't afford the photocopying, buy a banda machine on Ebay.

## Variations on a theme

- Use it as a tool for getting them to capture and make notes on their favourite moments in the film after they've just watched it in class, or on the coach home after a visit to the theatre so that they have a foundation for review writing in the next lesson.

- Get them using storyboards to remember the most important moments or artefacts or whatever they've just experienced, in sequence, on an educational trip.

- Use them to plan biographical or autobiographical writing. They visualise the most interesting 'scenes' of a person's life. Then get them exploring what scenes will be needed to join this together into a connected and interesting narrative.

## Whizzing it

Get the school/college digital video cameras out and let them see how well their visual script works in practice. Lots of mileage for critical evaluation to develop understanding of how narrative or any kind of dramatic presentation works.

# Summarising

## Taking the pith

## The basic idea

Take any text. Read it, identify the main points, present them in a concise form appropriate to purpose. Summarising is not easy. Like essay writing it can only be developed through practice, and through engagement with interesting tasks that require its use. Because it is challenging, and has an 'old-fashioned' stigma attached to it, what is called summarising is often nothing more than the reductive activity of completing a cloze exercise. Do it properly!

## Applying it

- Get students summarising speeches from a play in haiku form, as in Teachit's **Key Stage 3/4>Drama> Richard III>Act 1>Class activies for lines 1-41**.

- To build summarising skills, have students selecting the ten sentences from a non-fiction text that they think convey the most important ideas. Then they have to rewrite the ten sentences in such a way that they form a 100 word paragraph, with links between ideas and grammatical and stylistic fluency. Exactly 100 words.

- Another technique is to use a pyramid diagram. In the apex they write the most important idea in the text; in the next row the key supporting points; and in the bottom any examples that are necessary to make these points make sense. Then they write it up as a paragraph.

- For more support, use a summary grid, as in Teachit's resource **Key Stage 4>Prose>The Withered Arm by Thomas Hardy>Plot summary grid**.

- Get students writing two- to three-sentence scene or chapter summaries at the top of each scene – individually or collectively.

- On a smaller scale, write plot summaries of films (with no spoilers) as part of the process of writing detailed film reviews, or blurbs for DVD cases.

- Use summarising skills in 'real' tasks, such as summarising a 90-minute football match for a 90-second news report; produce a short general interest print news article summarising a specialist report into something interesting – *New Scientist* into *Daily Mail*, for example.

## What's the point?

Summarising is a very useful skill in a world where millions of pages of information on a topic can be accessed at the touch of a Google button. It encourages careful discrimination of key information, the ability to rework grammatical constructions to shape a new text, and concise expression. It involves complex critical thinking.

### Tricks of the trade

To make summarising accessible for the full ability range, there are a number of tricks you can use. Grids and pyramids can be partly filled in to help the less confident get started. Getting students to select the ten (or whatever) most important sentences in a text and then voting on them can encourage debate and develop better judgement of relevant ideas

### Variations on a theme

- Giving students a non-negotiable word or time length turns it into a bit of a *Krypton Factor* challenge, which adds a pleasing bit of spice for your puzzle-minded problem-solvers.

- Go grand scale and telly mad. Get them devising the schedule for one day (or one week if you're feeling ambitious) for a new digital channel of their choice to be launched. Then they have to produce the TV guide, summarising a selection of programming highlights and writing a couple of feature articles introducing readers to specific series or films they might be unfamiliar with (including, of course, summaries…). Use a range of telly guides as style models and then let them loose.

### Whizzing it

Get them producing summaries in Word and tracking the changes they have made so they can see each other's amendments more easily in discussion. Then they can use the word count function too – saves hours of adding up when you've set a fixed word length!

# Thinking hats

De Bono's thing

## The basic idea

Six hats each of a different colour, each representing one type of thinking. See table to the right.

Get students wearing the hats and doing the thinking, individually, in groups, as a class. If wearing hats is beyond the pale, flash them up on your big screen if working whole class, or have hat cards on desks for students to 'play' as they think, or a set of hats Blu-Tacked to your board. The hats can be worn/played in any order, and as many times as they are needed, but each hat must be used at least once in the process.

| White | Neutral thinking – facts, data, information |
|-------|---------------------------------------------|
| Red | Emotional 'gut reaction' thinking with no judgement or justification |
| Black | Critical judgement of ideas |
| Yellow | Positive perspectives and possibilities |
| Green | New ideas and creative alternatives |
| Blue | Control of the thinking process |

For a fuller description of the kind of thinking that goes with each hat, see **http://www.cs.unb.ca/profs/fritz/cs3503/sixhat35.htm**.

### Applying it

• Great for developing more sophisticated ideas in problem-solving tasks based on issues – i.e. what should be done about global poverty, identity theft, sex, drugs and rock'n'roll. Free flowing discussion with hats on and off. Get them summarising it and they've got 80% of an essay plan already.

• Useful for analysing crisis-point decisions characters have to make in texts. Outline the scenario, either before reading the text or when you get to the crunch point. Get students hat-wearing to decide what the best course of action would be. Explore, empathise, compare and contrast with what the writer chooses.

• Try it for opening up fresh literary interpretations. Worked really well in getting students past James Winny's received wisdom on the characters in the Chaucer's *General Prologue to the Canterbury Tales*. See 'No Rules Chaucer' in the December 2005 edition of *emagazine* for an account of this lesson with an A2 Literature class.

### What's the point?

Instead of thinking about issues or problems or ideas in a murky haze, this process separates out the types of thinking to be brought to bear on them, and says hey, let's just do one at a time. This can bring clarity of thought to a situation, and by ensuring that different types of thinking are used, greater depth and a sounder conclusion. It gives a framework for more disciplined discussion as only one hat is worn at a time.

### Tricks of the trade

Good verbal instruction is important, especially the first time you or the students are doing this. Doing it as a whole class activity is good the first time, so they can get the hang of it together. After that, it usually helps to have a simple reminder sheet on desks. In groups, nominate one person to wear the blue hat, then they get to keep the process under control and decide which hat needs to be played when. Then let them get on with it, trying as hard as you can not to interfere in their thinking process. Support the blue hats if needed and otherwise just listen – let them figure the ideas out themselves otherwise you've instantly defeated the whole object of the activity...

### Variations on a theme

• You put the blue hat on and control the process very strictly, giving a set time limit for each type of thinking in turn. Limits creative freeflow deliberately in favour of rapid brainstorming of ideas. These can then be developed more freely in open discussion.

# Thinking keys

Thinking upside down and inside out

## The basic idea

Thinking is a good thing, but classroom thinking can often run in rather narrow straight line grooves. To develop original, critical and creative ideas, students need to practise thinking in a wide variety of ways. Tony Ryan created the 'Thinker's Keys': Google it and you'll find downloads and explanations galore. The 'Thinkers Keys' include very familiar types of thinking, such as exploring disadvantages and alternatives, but it also includes intriguing types such as exploring apparently ridiculous ideas and finding commonality between unexpected objects. Don't be put off by the primary/middle school focus; these work with all age groups.

Download the booklet 'Thinker's Keys for Kids' at
**www.headfirst.com.au>
Thinkers Keys Free Material>
Thinkers Keys for Kids**

### Applying it

- Build a range of thinking types, one at a time, into your scheme of work. It doesn't matter that the students aren't going to be asked to construct a model in the exam, the classroom process of creative thinking and imaginative engagement with the text or topic will generate ideas worth writing down in an exam.

- Use the examples in the download to create your own sheets of 20 ways of thinking about a text or topic. Give students, individually or in groups, the opportunity to explore the topic with that thought process, or several of them, and see where they end up. Works well with all the kinds of non-fiction 'issues' set at GCSE.

- Once students are familiar with the thinker's keys, give them a blank grid and get them thinking up their own ideas for approaching the text or topic in each way.

### What's the point?

Thinking in narrow straight line grooves may help squeeze a few more students through whatever threshold is considered desirable in the latest test series, but it bores strong students rigid, does little to help weaker students and does nothing meaningful for any student's future progression.

Incorporating more kinds of thinking in the classroom will better equip students with tools for the problems and questions they face outside the classroom. Shifting between different modes of thinking encourages valuable flexibility. It also opens up new dynamics, in which students who find traditional academic modes of thinking difficult are often liberated by new approaches to the same problem and start showing the potential you knew was in there somewhere. Looking at issues from different angles often produces original ideas and anything that brings variety to the long slog of an academic year is good for students and definitely good for teachers.

### Tricks of the trade

This is one of those things that if you like it, you'll probably find all kinds of ways of using it and it'll end up informing all of your practice. It's not so much a 'thing to do next Wednesday' as a fundamental pedagogical practice. For that reason, it's best not to treat it as a 'thing to do next Wednesday' as it can be a bit overwhelming for students in one hit, especially if it's their first encounter with more divergent modes of thought. Better to build it up gradually unless your students used these all the time in primary school and are completely au fait with it all. This can also give you a chance to get used to the more divergent modes of thinking and to work out ways of channelling the ideas it produces.

### Variations on a theme

- Explore examples of different kinds of thinking. Terry Jones' work on Chaucer is wonderfully divergent. *The Knight's Tale* starts with the question, 'What if the knight isn't the paragon of virtue everyone thinks he is?', while *Who Murdered Chaucer?* builds an interesting argument from the equally speculative 'What if Chaucer didn't just disappear from the records but was murdered?'

# Thought tracking

## Dealing with divided selves and two-faced weasels

## The basic idea

Students are in pairs. They have a script or a section of dialogue. One person speaks the words actually used by the character, the other says what they are really thinking. Do it as a quick spontaneous way of brainstorming ideas, or as a practised and rehearsed performance with other characters.

### Applying it

- Characters with dark swirling undercurrents of evil work really well, so get straight on the case with those dastardly Macbeths. A couple of Teachit resources do this with fill-in thought bubbles – use as preparation or as an alternative for the camera-shy. Try **Key Stage 3/4>Drama> Macbeth – Act 1>Lady Macbeth's evil thoughts** and **Key Stage 3/4>Drama>Macbeth – Act2>Act2 Scene 1 – The serpent under the innocent flower**. Iago is another classic for this activity.

- Also try it with honest characters who are adopting a role or having to dissemble or are constrained by circumstances or social situation. Try Elizabeth Bennett and Mr Darcy saying what they really think in key scenes in *Pride and Prejudice*. Or Cordelia letting rip in the map scene in *King Lear*.

### What's the point?

It makes tangible what is encoded within and between the lines, and can draw out really interesting insights into the way individual students are reading the situation. For students who loathe drama activities, this can be a relatively pain free lesson that still gets them up on their feet, inside a character's head, and involved in a mini performance. Likewise for English teachers who loathe drama activities. Even I can manage this one....

### Tricks of the trade

Encourage experimentation with different possibilities rather than the first thing that comes to mind, as the first go can be a bit flat. To develop it, have a practice go together, all being one character with one or two lines. Then leave them to develop and extend it as far into the scene or dialogue as they can or want to. Lots of talking, and possibilities for shouting and screaming (depending on the level of repression the character is facing, of course, not gratuitous shouting and screaming), so another perfect back field lesson. Or another break time with no cuppa because you're hiding from your neighbouring teacher. Get a flask. It's worth it...

### Variations on a theme

- Instead of working from script or dialogue, explore the idea of thought tracking and get students improvising their own scenarios. Build up to imaginative writing.

- To prepare for the lesson, invite observation of scenarios and situations from real life or TV in which people aren't saying what they are really thinking. Use to start the lesson with a rich pool of ideas and examples.

### Whizzing it

Use the fill-in thought bubbles approach as in the *Macbeth* resources listed. Have the scene up on the IWB and have students adding their own thought bubbles to build a rich sense of alternative ideas and readings.

# Time lines

At last, a legitimate classroom use for Velcro

## The basic idea

Take any kind of knowledge with a chronological sequence. Get students researching what happened when and putting it in order, or give them the information for sequencing. Stick things on the wall in a timeline. Hang them on a washing line with pegs. Attach them to a strip of Velcro. Produce illustrated timeline wallcharts. Move information around on your IWB. A timeless classic.

## Applying it

- In its simplest form, simply sequence the events of a text in order, as for *Skellig* in Teachit's resource **Key Stage 3>Prose>Skellig by David Almond>Timeline of events**.

- More sophisticated activity can be had using a timeline to show how things change over time in a text, e.g. relationships as in Teachit's **Key Stage 4>Prose>To Kill A Mockingbird by Harper Lee>The changing relationship of Jem and Scout**.

- Unravel a novel with a more complex narrative structure, to put the events in chronological sequence, as in Teachit's **Key Stage 5>Prose>The Handmaid's Tale by Margaret Atwood>Timeline**.

- To explore literary language change, take a selection of texts and get students putting them into a timeline as in Teachit's resource **Key Stage 5>Skills>Introductory activities>The dating game**. For a wider range of texts, use the British Library's 'Texts in Context' at **www.bllearning.co.uk/live/text**.

## What's the point?

Sequencing is about the logical ordering of information, but creating a timeline goes beyond that, as it enables students to get the big picture of a topic or situation. Visualising it chronologically can help students to see patterns and connections that may be obscured when everything is in its own context. It can also be a great way to liven up your classroom walls.

### Tricks of the trade

Have rich and interesting texts to work with that will 'snag' on students' imaginations and lead to discussion beyond the simple act of sequencing. Build outwards from the basic task, getting students to add images, descriptions of important contextual influences, and any system they like of showing patterns and connections running through the chronology. Think big!

### Variations on a theme

- Individuals or small groups can each produce a timeline, or you can have them each producing a panel in it. The former encourages overview, the latter encourages depth of focus. Either way it's worth counterbalancing with a follow-up activity of the opposite kind.

- Undertaken collaboratively as a class, this kind of 'big' project can be good for getting different students working on tasks according to their interests and capabilities. Give someone project management responsibility as that talent doesn't always get much of an outing.

### Whizzing it

For a simple six or nine event timeline template, check out **www.teach-nology.com >Tools>Free Worksheet Makers>Time Line Generators**.

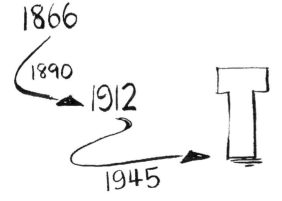

# Treasure hunt

## Collect stuff, answers, or photos

## The basic idea

You lay a physical trail. Students go round it following the arrows, picking up clues, solving problems, collecting tools that might be useful further along the way, and gradually working their way towards the educational treasure. They might collect physical objects, or stamps, or answers, or take photos of items on the trail. They might have a treasure map that has to be followed in order, or an orienteering circuit where each post must be visited at some point. There might be a time limit or a competitive element, there might not. But whatever format, the trail ends in a spot marked X where everything comes together and your students are the richer for it.

### Applying it

• My favourite technique for teaching students how to make the best use of the library for the study of English. Okay, so you need a smiling librarian to do it, but if you've got one, they are at least part of the treasure the students find…

• Museums are sometimes good at this for trips, but you often have to do it yourself if you want something specific. Ring most museums, take a school letter and you'll usually get in free (and if not, take your students elsewhere). I've spent several very pleasant afternoons lying on the grass while post-AS students did a treasure trail about language change at Pevensey Castle.

• If that's too much preparation, try this very simple treasure hunt: set students the challenge of finding (and of course justifying) the one thing in the exhibition that they would most like to take home. Erm, just make sure they know it's only a game…

• That kind of virtual treasure hunt also works well on a smaller scale as a conclusion to the study of a set text. If you could only keep one passage of the novel, or one poem, or one scene, which would it be? Often yields rich and surprising results.

### What's the point?

In its physical form of running around a trail, it allows the expression of physical energy as a valid tool for learning, and that can be very powerful for students who find sitting behind a desk all day a tough challenge. In all its forms, it can support the development of aesthetic judgement and the ability to discriminate finely between objects or texts of similar merit.

### Tricks of the trade

Don't do it if it's going to result in chaos because then learning won't take place and the glowering librarian/head of department/curator/caretaker will be justified. But if your students will follow instructions reasonably, then the key trick is to make sure the treasure is good and the puzzles are suitably challenging. Pair up younger or less able students, and/or differentiate trails. What you don't want is the super-keen doing it properly and everyone else borrowing their answers. Also think carefully about what treasure is. Chocolate isn't. Getting a library ticket or a book token or a free family ticket to the museum might be…

### Variations on a theme

• Get students to construct a treasure trail that is related to a writer or a particular book or something about local language, especially if you live somewhere with interesting connections. This is a good instructional writing task. The treasure might be a good café at the end…

• Over time, build up a bank of questions or problems, and give different groups different sets to solve. This can be a strategy for curing lazyitis, but it can also be about giving students things they will each find fun and challenging.

### Whizzing it

Give them a digital camera to record the answers with and use images in subsequent work, according to what you're trying to achieve by doing the trail. Could be used in presentations on what they would like to keep and why, or illustrating their own trail guide using Word or Publisher, or creating a virtual version of the trail for other people to use via the internet…

# True or false

The eternal question

## The basic idea

A nice easy teacher's favourite. Students get a series of statements about a character or a topic or a text. They have to decide if they are true or false. Do it individually or in groups, as a straightforward exercise or a whole class fun quiz, bits of paper or multimedia mayhem. Whatever rocks your boat.

### Applying it

- Do it as a straightforward true or false comprehension exercise, as in Teachit's resource on Malvolio's words and actions **Key Stage 3>Drama> Twelfth Night – Act 3 Scene 4>Work book 2**.

- Combine it with a card sort with students making heaps of true and false statements as in this Teachit activity **Key Stage 3>Drama> Macbeth – Act 1>Macbeth's soliloquy – true or false?**

- Soup it up a bit by making the statements true, false or debateable, as in this Teachit Flash resource on justice in *Measure for Measure*: **Key Stage 5>Drama>Measure for Measure>The theme of justice**.

### What's the point?

At a simple level, it is a useful little alternative to boring reading comprehension questions. It gets more interesting the more room for debate there is between the options, with different interpretations coming into play and much discussion of who is right and wrong. If you play your cards right you can also get into some important discussions about what truth is anyway. Just ask the question…

### Tricks of the trade

Make it worth a student bothering with, by asking some questions that need a bit of digging around to find the answers, or are unexpected in some way, or by including plenty of 'debateable' statements.

### Variations on a theme

- Try mixing it up as a game. I'm fond of doing it as a variation on the game of 'cheat'. Make true or false statement cards. Divide them out between students. They choose a card to play and try to pass it off as the truth. If the other students challenge them they can try to justify it. If they get away with it, they leave their card there, if not they have to take all the cards in the pile. The winner is the first person to get rid of all their cards. Works best with debateable statements; determining whether it is a 'cheat' or not is done by consensus debate.

- Follow the debateable ones up with more creative activities, such as turning the argument into a radio feature. Or use the true/false activity to identify the most contentious statement and set that up as a formal debate for next lesson.

### Whizzing it

Create an online true or false quiz yourself, or get students creating them, at sites like www.myquiz.net (though you will probably need to have a word with the school cyberpolice first to find out what they will let you use).

# Trump cards

Card game to assess characters' virtues/vices

## The basic idea

Students have a set of cards, based on the 'Top Trumps' game, which depict the characters from the text and assess their characteristics. This is done in one of two ways: either as qualities listed under headings like 'strengths' and 'special powers'; or as a fixed set of qualities on all the cards which are given a score out of ten to show the character's strength. E.g. moral virtue 9.37, dress sense 2.1. Or you can use a hybrid system.

Students then play the game. The cards are dealt out between the players. Player one chooses a card to play, and selects a feature s/he thinks will beat the others. Any student who thinks one of his/her cards can trump that says so and a debate takes place. It's a bit easy if everything has a score value, but if it's a question of whether, for example, patience beats kindness then you get interesting debates about the characters. Whoever wins, by consensus agreement, gets a card from all of the other players. The idea is to win all the cards (or as many as possible in a time limit).

## Applying it

- Works brilliantly with the pilgrims from Chaucer's *General Prologue* with loads of scope for exploring moral qualities, appearance, type of horse etc.

- Great in any novel involving monsters and supernatural powers. *Harry Potter and the Goblet of Fire*, *Harry Potter and the Prisoner of Azkaban*, Narnia, and Roald Dahl goodies and baddies 'Top Trumps' cards already exist for a ready-made lesson.

## What's the point?

Particularly if you use cards with descriptors rather than numerical scores, it engages students in raging debate about the relative status of different characters. It draws out the way the students perceive the characters which can lead into really good discussion of alternative interpretations of the text. Closeness in scores, or closely contested argument about which character wins, draws out similarities between characters, while easy wins highlight differences. The negotiation needed to win is an important oral skill, while the use of consensus to determine the outcome teaches a valuable social process.

## Tricks of the trade

It only works with a text with enough characters/cards to get a good game going. It is more lively in a group of four or five as more debate takes place, but don't make the groups too big or it can either get a bit out of hand or no-one gets enough cards to have fun. If you use cards with numerical scores, it will go very quickly and with little debate so I favour either quality descriptors or a hybrid scheme.

## Variations on a theme

- If you make or adapt the cards you are denying your students a large part of the fun and/or learning. So unless your purpose is limited to a quick game as a warm-up to something else, it's great getting the students to design and make the cards themselves. They determine the qualities to include, any scoring system, they can choose images to illustrate the cards, etc. Deep learning all round...

- If that's too time consuming there is a speedier version. Create laminated DIY sets of cards with boxes for strengths, special powers etc left blank. Give students a washable OHT pen (again yay for the retro-tech!). They fill in the boxes. Play the game. At the end of the lesson wipe clean and you're ready for the next class.

- 'Top Trumps' also has a set of horror cards which are useful (and glow in the dark – special bonus!) – neat, or the idea adapted - for exploring ideas about this type of genre fiction.

- Students can play the game with differing degrees of argumentative sophistication and textual knowledge. Consider differentiating groups to take account of this.

- Get students writing the cheat guide for this game, informing players how best to go about winning. Or challenge them to improve it or come up with an alternative if they think it's rubbish.

## Whizzing it

Set up a template for the cards on the network and give each student or pair the task of completing a certain number. Play, evaluate and redraft after discussion of whether the cards accurately reflected the relative strength of the characters in the text.

# Under pressure

Force field analysis diagrams

## The basic idea

Get students thinking about tension in any kind of situation by using a force field diagram. In this, the situation is represented in some way in the middle of the page, then arrows are used to represent the pressures that are acting upon it from different directions. Like this, where the arrows on the left represent the forces of evil, and those on the right the forces of good. Then let the discussion commence.

### Applying it

- Having modelled it with the scene from Macbeth shown below, invite students to select other scenes they think have a lot of tension and get them producing their own diagrams for these.

- Use it to explore the tension of Okwe's dilemma in Teachit's *Dirty Pretty Things* resource **Key Stage 3/4>Prose>Creative Writing2>A grotesque discovery**.

- Try it with the nanosecond before Frankenstein brings his creature to life, or his decision about whether or not to create a female partner for it.

*(continued over)*

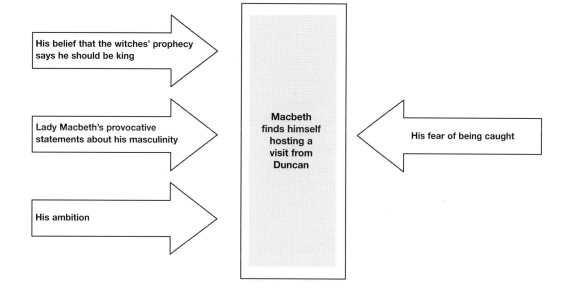

His belief that the witches' prophecy says he should be king

Lady Macbeth's provocative statements about his masculinity

His ambition

Macbeth finds himself hosting a visit from Duncan

His fear of being caught

### What's the point?

It gets students debating the moral forces at work in any situation, and that's a good thing, quite irrespective of the useful insights it sheds on literary tension. It makes tangible different interpretations of the scene or situation, as different numbers of arrows will reveal different readings. It provides a snapshot of the tension at any given moment, which can be used to develop ideas about narrative structure, exploring what action, dialogue or description created that tension, and how the writer goes on to release it.

### Tricks of the trade

If students haven't encountered this technique before, it might be a good idea to do it the first time as a whole class activity, or to model it first. It's a visual thing, so I like to go the whole hog on that, with flipchart paper and coloured markers so we can all share what's been produced afterwards. That also makes it a more physical activity, keeping your creative scribblers and fiddlers happy for hours. Well, okay, maybe not hours… Then it's all about the quality of the follow through. Get them finding quotations to support the points on their arrows, presenting their readings to the class, discussing questions about how the writer has created this tension using those deceptively simple little things, words.

### Variations on a theme

• Use the arrows to represent any opposing moral forces it is useful to explore, not just good and evil. Doubt and certainty, hope and fear, courage and cowardice – whatever works in your text.

• Go multi-dimensional, with arrows coming in from different directions to show multiple moral forces at work. Nice if you get different groups working on a different pair of forces, then build a multi-dimensional model as a class.

• Get students experimenting with different thicknesses of arrows to represent the differing significances of the forces identified.

• Also try it for development of persuasive argument, putting a controversial premise in the box, and using arrows to represent arguments for and against.

• Try the dramatic version of this technique, 'Conscience Alley'. In this, two lines of students form facing each other. These could represent two conflicting streams of thought inside a character's mind; opposing views of a character; two sides of a dilemma; or different characters' hostile views of another character. Then one student in role as the key character walks down the alley, as the students forming its walls whisper or shout out their comments. See *NATE Drama Packs* for examples of this technique in action and/or Teachit's Macbeth resource **KS3/4>Drama>Macbeth: a Drama scheme>Three ghosts visit Macbeth**.

### Whizzing it

Deep joy on an interactive whiteboard or PCs: get clicking those autoshapes. Let your clicker-happy students fill their arrows with colour for maximum technophilic ecstasy.

# Using corpora

Very cool language gizmo

## The basic idea

This is a technique for analysing and exploring language that is more usually found in HE, but there is no reason why they should have all the fun. It's an emerging application, one to start tinkering with as it develops. But basically, here's how it goes. You take one big body of language – that's the corpus – something like a whole text, or the British National Corpus with its 100 million word sample of very late 20th century English. Then you use a bit of software to do really cool, quick and powerful kinds of analysis of this body of language.

The simplest format is to use the free online edition of the British National Corpus. Everything you need is right here at **www.natcorp.ox.ac.uk**. Type in a word or phrase you want to interrogate in the 'look up' box of the 'Search the Corpus' section in the middle of the page. It will return a random sample of 50 uses of this word and tell you how frequently it occurs in the 100 million word corpus.

There are many other tools for corpus analysis and ways of using it but they are beyond the scope of this book. This is just a little taster of what's to come!

### Applying it

- Use this technique to get students exploring the connotations of colour words. They type in a colour, get the 50 hits, then explore the range of ideas and attitudes that are being represented by this word. Nice...

- Use it to explore synonymy in more detail. Get students to explain the difference, from the 50 hit evidence, between fast, rapid and quick.

- Or for language change, get them exploring those Old English, Norman French and Latin triplets as they are used in modern English, e.g. kingly, royal and regal.

- Sick of explaining the difference between there, their and they're to no avail? Get students examining 50 examples of each and telling you what the difference is! Or cut and paste the hits into Word and mix them up to get students examining them more closely.

### What's the point?

It can present ideas about language more powerfully to students because you are looking at real examples, not made up neat and tidy text book examples to which the eternal cry is 'Yeah but, what about...?' It gets students interrogating evidence for themselves in order to formulate ideas, encouraging in the process close attention to detail, the ability to see patterns, classification and definition skills. For students who always need to see it for themselves rather than take it on trust from a teacher, this can be a very powerful approach to learning.

### Tricks of the trade

If you have a fast internet connection this is exciting stuff for paired work on a PC. If your school/college is on some dodgy connection out of the ark, don't bother as you'll end up with a headache from trying to manage thirty frustrated students with nothing to do while they're waiting for their 50 hits to come up. In that case, use pre-prepared print-outs and start advocating hard for decent equipment you can actually use in a classroom. Useful to have these as back-up anyway in case Transco drill through your main cable mid-lesson, as they do... (Especially if you're being observed or inspected!)

### Variations on a theme

- If straightforward analysis of the hits is a bit challenging, try using the corpus generated examples to create a very grounded cloze exercise – beats trying to think up sufficient real examples of their, there and they're.

# Venn diagrams

## To explore similarities between characters

## The basic idea

Take any two items which you want to compare and contrast. Two newspaper articles taking different positions on a story; two characters in a text; two dialects; two poems on a similar theme; two whole texts for the development of comparative coursework essay title ideas. Students draw a Venn diagram and fill it with notes to show the differences between the two things as well as what lies in the overlap.

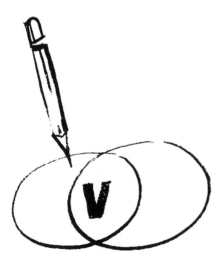

## Applying it

- Teachit's resource **Key Stage 3> Poetry>Comparing poems>Comparing poems pack** has students working on William Blake's 'Tyger! Tyger!' and Ted Hughes' 'View Of A Pig'. Use Venn diagrams to develop a strong sense of comparison of key points.

- For anthology revision, have students drawing any two poems/texts out of a lucky dip bag of whichever anthology you're working on. Their challenge is to find fresh, meaningful and interesting overlaps.

- Compare pairs of characters in *Othello*: Desdemona and Emilia; Iago and Roderigo; Cassio and Othello; Iago and Desdemona. All sorts of interesting connections start emerging.

## What's the point?

It develops comparative analysis. Using a visual record of this gives a tangible focus to the discussion and supports those students who prefer to 'see' an idea. It is a useful technique for the first stages of comparative essay planning. When exploring character in literary texts, it often opens up really interesting and creative lines of enquiry, especially if you encourage students to try out less obvious character pairings. It doesn't matter if they find no common ground: that is still fruitful matter for discussion and besides, it's both more exciting and more creative to try ideas out without worrying whether or not they'll work.

### Tricks of the trade

Can be useful to show students an example of what you're after if they are likely to run screaming at a teensy bit of Maths terminology.

### Variations on a theme

- Get students putting the Venn diagram at the centre of a poster illustrating the two characters for a nice bit of open evening preparation.

- For an extra challenge dimension, get students using three overlapping circles. This way they have to find the overlaps between pairs of circles and between all three. Or do a Venn chain as a class!

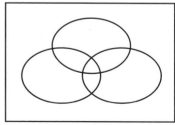

### Whizzing it

Venn diagrams come oven-ready in the diagram tool in Word (in the Insert menu). Do them together on the interactive whiteboard or in pairs in the PC suite. Easy.

# Verbal collage

The spine-shivering effect of choral speaking

## The basic idea

Students work in groups to select their favourite lines from the text you've just finished reading. In a circle, the first person reads the first favourite line aloud, then the second person the second, and so on round until all the lines have been spoken. Then they start overlapping the lines so that there aren't any gaps. When they've got the hang of that, they start experimenting with ways of turning this into an interesting spoken performance. They might mix the lines up, try them at different speeds, add other sound effects, try different vocal approaches - whatever they can think up. Perform. Discuss.

### Applying it

• Ghost stories provide multiple spooky noise opportunities for a simple application that can help explore the way voice can convey tension and fear. Try whispering, shouting, fast and slow – what combination is the scariest?

• Try it with an anthology of First World War texts: you need to have explored a wide enough range of texts to develop richness and variety in the spoken performance, but if you have it works very well.

• Works well with any text with cracking one-liners and powerful voices – *King Lear* and *1984* are both tried and tested spine-chillers with this activity.

### What's the point?

Selection entails discrimination on the grounds of aesthetic qualities that have to be debated and agreed as a group. That's a pretty good start, to which you can add the development of creative thinking and the often neglected development of a feeling for the aural texture of language. Students have to exercise excellent teamwork skills in order to pull off a performance of this kind in which timing is crucial. Students create interpretations of the text which can be compared and analysed after the main event.

### Tricks of the trade

Have a trial go as a whole class first so that students get the gist of what you want them to achieve. Then keep out of the creative experimentation process as much as you can, other than to keep a basic sense of order. Experimenting with sound will and must involve volume and screeching at some point, so think about where and when it's best to do this activity. The back field on a summer's day is good...

### Variations on a theme

• Try it with lines from a series of related news articles on an emotive topic like a major disaster – can be cathartic in giving young people an outlet through which to express their feelings without them having to attempt any logical analysis of it.

• For a much shorter version, do it with a key scene or chapter. More constrained, less to discuss, but very useful as a way of exploring mood.

### Whizzing it

If you've got time (nice languid summer term thing to do), get them researching additional sound effects to use in digital audio recordings. Build into a magazine programme on the topic and podcast it to the world.

# Visits

Few top tips

## The basic idea

Get out of the classroom! As simple as that. Well, as simple as that once you've done the risk assessment, the letters, the parental consents, the money, the delicate justification in triplicate of why this is an essential educational experience, etc etc. No two ways about it: a bureaucratic headache. But always worth it on the day.

### Applying it

• Take students to stadium gigs like 'Poetry Live!' and 'Sovereign' lectures for A Level students. Pile 'em high events that some people like.

• A trip to a performance of the text is a great experience, especially for students who would not otherwise have the opportunity to go to the theatre. Bung in a schools workshop where they get to work with actors and you've got a great day out. Check out your local theatre as well as your show-stoppers like The Globe.

• Art galleries can be great places for creative writing workshops, but then so too can some hills. A colleague ran a successful enrichment programme for several years with students out walking on the South Downs and writing poetry. Very Wordsworth, very inspirational.

• Go with any number of school visit packages in museums and galleries. Most large institutions and many quite modest ones have an education team. They'll have a set of workshops for

different key stages that you can opt into. Sometimes they're free! Worth trawling around the websites of different places to get a flavour of the kinds of thing on offer, but talking to the education officer often uncovers many more things, and some will do custom packages.

• Create your own package. Most places let teachers in free for reconnaissance visits. Of course, in most of the rest of the EU – ahem, world - teachers never have to pay the full admission price for museums and galleries, and quite rightly so. But hey-ho… Ring up, tell them what you're doing and make an appointment to visit. Take proof: a brief 'to whom it may concern' on headed paper confirming that you teach at your school. Sometimes you go round with the education officer, sometimes they leave you to your own devices.

• This is a useful starting point: **www.24hourmuseum.org.uk** and worth checking in with on a regular basis to see what's new in the museums world.

## What's the point?

Being stuck inside the same four walls every day is no fun for anyone, including teachers. At its most basic, doing something different gets us all out of a rut, and that can bring new energy and fresh thinking to whatever it is that you're doing. It's cheesy but also true that a trip bonds a class as nothing else can, though if you want the full monty on that you either have to do a residential or have a truly terrible experience. But the most important thing is the richness of learning that can take place once the institutional straitjacket is off. The bell doesn't go every forty minutes; students have contact with inspirational artefacts, experts and experiences; and the environment is special in some way. Powerful stuff.

## Tricks of the trade

Get as many adult bodies on board as you can: the higher the ratio the better. How? Some people go for parents but they make me a bit nervous in case I accidentally drop their child, so I prefer to invite language assistants, PGCE students and NQTs. They'll be CRB checked too.

Fill all the paperwork in properly, however tedious. Risk assessments can be ridiculous in some places, but you must stop laughing long enough to think about meeting points, emergency contact, and how you're going to manage the not entirely unlikely scenario of losing a student. Pick an adult other than you to be in charge of blood, vomit and inhalers (no point keeping a dog and barking yourself), and brief a nominated second-in-command in case you choke to death on an Eccles cake.

Make sure the activities are worth doing and appropriately challenging for all students, and that there is time and space built in for both letting off a bit of steam and shopping. Neglect student opportunities to buy their mums a souvenir and you'll never hear the end of it.

In the lesson before you go, make sure every student in the class understands your expectations of behaviour. This is no time for shilly-shallying around pretending to be their friend: be crystal clear about the rules (but don't have more than three) and threaten them with death if they break them. Make sure you know how you will deal with any infringement, and don't set rules you can't uphold. Like most things in teaching, good planning and clear boundaries maximise the opportunity for everyone to have a great time. Enjoy it!

## Variations on a theme

- Instead of going out to a museum, get them to come into your classroom. Create a virtual museum, with exhibits mounted around the classroom or hall or other space. Set students off on a virtual visit.

- For the full monty, go residential, but preferably not until you've first done a few with old hands in the lead roles so that you can get the full measure of the thing. Stratford is perennially popular, Arvon writing courses in Devon, the First World War battlefields for poetry readings, but there are zillions of possibilities – you don't have to be a Geographer to go on a field trip…

- Start your own museum – how cool is that? A downloadable pack to get you started is here: **www.24hourmuseum.org.uk>***For teachers>Museum in a Classroom*.

## Whizzing it

Lots of museums and galleries have their collections available online. Get students visiting the collection from the comfort of your own IT suite. Not the same, but useful when you've used up your personal allocation of trip days.

# Voting
## Techniques to liven it up

## The basic idea

Picking the best idea, the most persuasive argument, the most interesting character, the best scene, etc, can spark intense and useful debate. Let it run for a while, naturally, but if you want to bring it to some kind of conclusion, throwing it out to a vote can be useful in several ways. One person, one vote is the usual format. Secret ballot or hands in the air according to time and/or predilection. But for the full fat with sugar super grande mocha latte with whipped cream experience, go for a mock election.

### Applying it

• As a pre-reading task for utopian/dystopian fiction for both GCSE and A Level, students prepare 'If I ruled the world' manifestos, present them at classroom hustings, and then vote in the classroom 'Ruler of the World' who reigns for the duration of the scheme of work and is called upon periodically to deliver his/her verdict on the events in whatever story or novel you are reading. *Gulliver's Travels… 1984… The Handmaid's Tale… I Robot…*

• The whole kingship election in *Macbeth* is intriguing. We only hear second hand about Macbeth being named as king, and likewise Malcolm once Macbeth's head is in the bag. Makes a neat little activity to role play the succession meeting of the thanes with a vote at the end, the former helping to explore Macbeth's public image at the time of Duncan's death, the latter the ending of the play and what it means.

### What's the point?

For the speaker or writer it can help to develop persuasive argument and rhetorical skill. For the electorate, it encourages decisive judgement and can give rise to valuable discussion about the nature of decisions made in this way. Start this discussion the minute the howls of 'it's not fair' go up! Important stuff…

### Tricks of the trade

Hands in the air is quick and easy, but a secret ballot will often produce more interesting results as you don't get students voting like sheep. It also heightens the drama of the occasion. To maximise this, appoint a couple of ballot counters and have a Returning Officer declare the result in an appropriately rhetorical style.

### Variations on a theme

• Can also be used for peer evaluation. After a group work exercise, get students to vote in a secret ballot on who made the most effort in the activity. Award 'man of the match' status/prizes in each group. Yes, yes, or 'woman' or 'person'…

• If you're having issues with some students freeloading off others in group activities, bide your time until voting is a useful strategy on a topic all the students really want to have their say on. Then get evil teacher revenge by giving loaded votes. One vote to students who have made little effort, two to those who have consistently tried, and three to students who have consistently pushed beyond their limits. Even better, do it on ruthlessly objective grounds, according to progress review grades, or unauthorised absence. The ultimate – get them to give their peers a score of 1-3 for effort, and then award voting rights accordingly. You can only do it once but boy is it fun. And then obviously do some highly professional and educationally important work on self-evaluation and target setting…

### Whizzing it

If your school/college has those fancy vote zapper things for your interactive whiteboard, get them out and play with them. Hours of family entertainment.

# Watching telly

Go on, you know you want to...

## The basic idea

Watch telly – documentaries, films, soaps, adaptations, productions of the set text, poetry readings, whatever... So easy it doesn't even feel like a pedagogical technique. Except when someone's left a video jammed in the machine, or the DVD skips, or your classroom telly sets on fire when you plug it in...

### Applying it

• Watching the film all the way through without worrying about the quality of the thinking can be a good thing as it gives students an important whole text dramatic experience. Maximise that wherever possible with the biggest screen you can lay your hands on, preferably in a setting where students aren't sitting on hard plastic chairs behind desks, and even more preferably without the school bell going just as you're getting to the best bit. Beg/borrow/steal cash and rent your local cinema for a private screening for a couple of hundred quid.

• When working on individual sections or scenes of texts, get your techies to make you a compilation of extracts from different productions for comparative work. Get students logging certain details as they watch and then comparing and contrasting.

• Set comprehension style questions for watching documentaries, as long as students can still see the page when you flick off the house lights. Help them keep track by putting questions under time counter headings. Pause after each section to allow students to compare answers and fill in gaps before moving on. See **Zombie killers** (on page 150) for other ideas.

• Get students making notes to produce a lively critical review of whatever it is they're watching. Get them inventing the categories, such as relevance to study at this level, best idea, best bit, best line of dialogue, most cringeworthy moment, etc. Produce individual or collective reviews, have a class vote on marks out of ten overall, and slap it on a sticker on the DVD/video. Useful future reference for you/other teachers and it gets all the groaning dealt with so you can move on to serious discussion of the ideas.

### What's the point?

Pressing the on button is usually the easy bit. The challenge is to keep everyone awake, alert and engaged in thinking about what they're watching. Well, most of the time anyway – sometimes watching telly is a useful survival strategy...

### Tricks of the trade

Always test the equipment in someone else's classroom, test it twice when you're being observed/inspected and always test the video/DVD you are going to use. If that's a shared departmental resource, padlock it to your wrist on the day you plan to use it and always have a contingency for technical disaster because it will happen. Regularly.

### Variations on a theme

• Get students selecting relevant viewing material themselves. For media tasks for GCSE and for AS language study, the student task of choosing mini packages of TV ads – from source or from a provided pool – has kept me in beautifully produced teaching resources for years...

### Whizzing it

Record clips of programmes in a digital media format, save to the network, and get students watching them (with headphones) at their own pace, in their own order, and with as many replays as are feasible. Give them some questions to answer or a task to complete and they'll be busy clicking and watching for ages.

# Webquest

Adventures in cyberspace and/or the ICT suite

## The basic idea

Students get an extended opportunity to use the internet to conduct research into a topic or question. This is structured appropriately for age and stage, with a clearly defined outcome that requires them to process the large body of information they will have found – presentations, discussions, feature articles, whatever…

### Applying it

• Teachit has a generous and free-ranging Key Stage 3 Shakespeare webquest at **Key Stage 3>Drama> Introduction to Shakespeare: background and biography>Will Shakespeare Quill to Keyboard**.

• Exploring cultural context is a good use of this technique as there are so many avenues for students to explore. Teachit's *Let Him Have It!* scheme of work has a nice webquest on the 1950s cultural context to the debate about hanging at **Key Stage 4> Media & Non-Fiction>Let Him Have It!>British Society in the 1950s**.

• Also try Teachit's cultural context research project at **Key Stage 4> Prose>Dr Jekyll and Mr Hyde>Dr Jekyll and Mr Hyde – research topics**.

### What's the point?

This is about giving students a bit of freedom to explore things in the more natural way they do outside school,

where plenty of rich learning takes place. Though free-ranging it's not a free-for-all, but there is scope for students to explore things at their own pace and in ways that make intuitive sense to them. They can each follow very different lines of enquiry according to their interest and enthusiasm. Although they complete the same task, the outcomes can be very different, producing fertile grounds for comparative discussion. It supports the development of independent learning skills, and changes the student-teacher dynamic in interesting and productive ways by giving students an opportunity to become the expert for a change. Discussion naturally arises about effective use of the internet for research.

### Tricks of the trade

It's all in the planning. Set up an interesting higher order question that cannot be answered by a lucky landing on a single website. Then you need to provide clear written instructions to guide students through the issues and processes you want them to explore. For this, I like the DIY webquest generator template provided free at **www.teachnology.com >Worksheets>Free Worksheet Makers>Web Quest Generator**. Fill in the boxes, click on the button, and kerboom, your webquest instructions are ready to print. Then it's just the small matter of troubleshooting, chivvying along, issuing dire threats when they start online chat with their best mate, fixing the PC that's just crashed…

### Variations on a theme

• To speed it up or make it more accessible to less independent students, narrow the scope of the question and increase the prescriptiveness of the instructions. To soup it up, make the question a matter of careful judgement and give only a few starting points for research.

# Website DIY

Or, how not to do them, having learned the hard way...

## The basic idea

Students write and publish web pages on a text or topic.

### Applying it

- Get students writing a mini-website for year 6 pupils thinking of coming to the school with Teachit's comprehensive scheme of work **Key Stage 3>NLS Framework Page>Exploring information based websites (NLS Y7)**.

- Get students of any age or stage producing their own book review site using a free and easy website creation service like the very popular www.piczo.com. Agree a format they think is cool (that's several hours of really valuable debate about reading for a start...), produce a template, and then have students adding reviews of books they've read and enjoyed. Check out the competition at **www.cool-reads.co.uk**. Or their own illustrated interactive poetry anthology site...

- My AS Literature class produced a website on the 'Life and Times of Emily Bronte', exploring every aspect of context outlined in the AQA B specification. They each took one aspect, then they identified their own individual research focus and wrote one web page on it. Then we put it all together. Great bonding, great work...

### What's the point?

Real publication of work is immensely powerful in motivating students to produce something worth reading, and the internet doubles that because most students are highly familiar with it as a publication context. Electronic publishing is the future, and we should be making sure our students have some access to that, and to its literacy practices, as well as to the rich heritage of writing that it necessarily draws upon. It is also a very valuable learning experience for students to realise they know more about something than their teachers.

### Tricks of the trade

Don't be afraid of not knowing as much as your students. Set it up using a template to make it manageable, but if students have the technical skill to develop that further, let 'em. Chat up your IT teachers and technicians for advice about the best approach. I used a cheap bit of software with a mixed group of 8-15 year olds and it was simple enough for Word users, but, the teenage girls in the group laughed at me and showed me their far more sophisticated (and far pinker...) websites produced with piczo. Well worth the screaming fist-fight and/or quiet patient bribery needed to get the school cyberpolice on your side for this project.

### Variations on a theme

- Get them blogging at **www.blogger.com**. Use a team blog to publish creative writing by the whole class in a simple format, one that their friends and parents can view. Get them maintaining their own blogs about anything they are interested in and they will soon be writing regularly without even thinking about it. Another challenge for the school cyberpolice...

- Good idea to get them researching how different kinds of web pages present their information. There is no such thing as a writing frame for a web page because it is an emerging form with a huge amount of variation (hurrah!). Instead, get them finding examples of formats and ideas they like: not just font and colour, but ways of managing the discourse.

# Word bag

If only you could get the shoes to match

## The basic idea

In each lesson where you will be introducing lots of new vocabulary or terminology, nominate one student as the bag filler. His/her task is to record all of the new words, and their definitions, on separate blank word cards (index cards or similar). If there is going to be a lot, you might like to encourage entrepreneurial sub-contractual arrangements, but otherwise, pick on someone annoying and make them do it all (oops, sorry, that just slipped out, obviously I didn't mean that at all…). S/he drops the cards into the magic word bag as they are done, checking anything with you that isn't clear. Then you have everything you need for a terminology test or a spelling test or a vocabulary test for the rest of the class at the end of the lesson, or the start of the next one, or next February – just pull a word out of the bag and off you go.

## Applying it

- Works well with any kind of terminology – media, literature, language – and at any key stage.

- Instead of a random test, give the students a cloze exercise to do. You pull a word out of the bag, they have to figure out where it goes.

## What's the point?

First of all, it gets a student to take responsibility for a task. This is an important role to experience, so make sure you rotate it round the class over time. Sometimes it will be done more competently than others, but that doesn't matter – you can always tweak the cards if you need to, though if you encourage the right approach the student will check everything carefully first. You can always get the class to do the checking collectively. Encouraging responsibility for learning is important in insisting our students become something other than spoonfed milksops. In addition, this activity generates no-preparation resources for you to use in different ways in future lessons, and for students there is something valuable in gradually seeing the bag fill up – a tangible realisation of how much they have learned.

## Tricks of the trade

Don't accept sloppy work – insist on accuracy and checking by the individual and/or the class. Have nice cards and a groovy bag to keep the words in – a Tesco's carrier and some ripped up bits of scrap paper may work with some students in a retro-chic kind of way, but not many… I'm particularly fond of primary school book bags, myself – lovely colours, great Velcro.

### Variations on a theme

- Instead of putting the words straight into the bag, they could get stuck on the wall for a time, so that the class can absorb them more gradually. As new words are generated take the old ones off the wall, or invite students to vote for which words they are ready to have go in the bag.

### Whizzing it

You could do this with a virtual bag, but they don't come in nearly such nice fabrics…

# Wordsearch

Makes a change occasionally...

## The basic idea

Easy peasy lemon squeezy and nice for a change every now and again. You know the thing: words are hidden in a rectangle of letters and the object is to find them all, vertically, horizontally, diagonally, backwards or forwards, up or down, as quickly as possible. Easy wordsearch puzzles will give the words in a list at the bottom. Medium challenge puzzles will give the first letter and a series of spaces to show the number of letters in the word, or a series of questions to answer in order to identify the words to be found in the puzzle. Tougher puzzles don't give you anything except the number of words to be found that are related to the given topic.

## Applying it

- Teachit's resource **Key Stage 3>Poetry>The Pied Piper of Hamelin>Wordsearch** is a simple wordsearch. Extend it by getting students to do it and then write questions or a cloze activity to which the answer is one of the words. Of course you could start this way round, as in Teachit's **Key Stage 3/4>Drama>Twelfth Night>Fun Quiz and wordsearch activities – Act 2 Scene 5**.

- For simple memory-jogging of the text's basics for revision and/or an emergency cover lesson, see **Key Stage 4>Drama>An Inspector Calls by JB Priestley>Getting to know the play: crossword and wordsearch**.

- Use it to test recognition and understanding of terminology appropriate to any age or stage. Bury the words in the wordsearch. Their task is to find them and provide definitions.

### What's the point?

Even in its most basic form it can encourage concentration, attention to detail, and pattern recognition for spelling. And some students just really like doing puzzles. When it's souped up a bit with questions and definitions, more thinking is encouraged about the text or the words. If it becomes a central plank of your teaching repertoire, be worried, but as a way of mixing it up a bit, or just having a nice quiet starter activity for a change, it has definite uses.

### Tricks of the trade

Don't make it too easy or it's no fun at all. Puzzles are supposed to puzzle... But that doesn't mean to say *you* need to spend hours puzzling over it, so definitely use a free online word search generator as here **http://school.discovery.com >Puzzlemaker>Word Search**.

### Variations on a theme

- Try other puzzle options at the above website. Criss-Cross Puzzle is a crossword generator. Try putting key quotations into the Fallen Phrase puzzle generator or letter tiles. You can also turn them into code! Hours of fun.

- Don't hog all the fun: get students to make their own puzzles for future revision and/or mutual testing purposes.

### Whizzing it

Whack your puzzles up on the IWB and turn the lesson into big screen fun.

# Writing kick starts
## Teacher's Emergency Survival Box

## The basic idea

Everyone has their favourite: the little kick start for creative writing that you use on a rainy day when you've just finished *Macbeth* and the thought of the anthology is too awful to face just yet. Or when you just want to see what a new class can do. Or when you're covering someone else's lesson and the students say 'we've done that', or when you're just back from being off sick and need a simple little thing to ease you back into your stride with no preparation. Well, none, that is, if you've got a few of these things ready in your teacher's emergency survival box.

## Applying it

• Get the students playing 'Consequences' and then developing the products into short stories, dramas, or whatever they like. Go 'X-treme Consequences' with nine turns rather than five. Include settings, outfits, objects, pets, whatever…

• Have in your emergency box a selection of pictures of the weirdest and most wonderful items you can find on eBay. (Get a stalker-child to do this for you some time as a 'special project'.) Get students marvelling at them, discussing them and developing their backstories – how they ended up on eBay.

• Play progressive storytelling, in which you all sit in a nice round, you give students the opening line of a story (invented or from the nearest book you can reach), one starts the story off and keeps going for as long as they like/can, then the next student picks up the thread and carries on, and so on.

• Do wheely bin characterisation. Like those magazine features where they take photos of what's in slebs' dustbins, give students pictures of items in a character's bin. They write *Talking Heads* style monologues or 'A Life In the Day…'

• If one lesson isn't enough for getting back into your stride (and your class is vaguely sensible) make the next lesson a creative writing workshop session. Get them into groups and give them a constructive feedback frame such as 'What I liked about your piece was…' and 'The bit I wasn't so sure about was….' and 'I think it will end with…' Each group member gives these comments; discussion takes place; then have another class writing burst to build on the ideas generated.

## What's the point?

Schemes of work are beautiful things but sometimes you need a little trick up your sleeve for days when that just isn't going to happen. It's a survival strategy. If you go with oral storytelling instead of writing you have more work to do in the classroom but no homework to mark - important if you're doing this when you've just come back from illness or when you're covering another teacher's class.

The workshop process isn't just a filler: it treats drafting as a much more active and socially engaged process, where other people – who are both readers and writers – provide feedback and encouragement, and tell their own and alternative stories. Students are generally far more supportive of each other than we might expect, and they often come up with really cool ideas for each other's writing. It models a useful process of drafting rather than the mental model most students have of simply 'copying it up in neat'.

## Tricks of the trade

Pick weird, unusual and unexpected stuff in these activities to get students thinking imaginatively. Give students time to discuss their ideas, or think quietly about them, or draw a few doodly scribbles, but don't let them start writing straight away. Once they've had time to think, give a time limit in which to write. This might be a whole lesson, or it might be ten minutes. At the end of it they stop wherever they have got to, you move into discussion and further development, and then give them another burst of writing. Bursts are usually far more productive than the endless stretch…

## Variations on a theme

- Add an extra challenge dimension to the progressive storytelling activity by giving one student the first line of the story and another the last line; the class then has a responsibility to get the story from A to B.

- Get students writing character portraits in poetic form from their wheely bin contents and lining them up in a *General Prologue* style sequence. Get students to devise a narrative frame suited to the portraits and modern times.

- For further stimulus points ransack your local bookshop or library for creative writing handbooks. My current favourite is *The Pocket Muse* by Monica Wood. Cheesy Americana in places, but some nice starting points too e.g. write a story in which three objects exist at the beginning and only one at the end. Have a lucky dip bag of objects to get that one under way.

- For the workshop, you could make one student in each group responsible for facilitating their workshop. Give them clear instructions about their task. This means they won't get feedback on their writing, so you could either select those who perhaps need feedback least, or those who are most reluctant to share their work (facilitating the discussion is no cop-out as they'll soon find!). Their task should also be to feedback to the whole class on what they found interesting about the process and what was learned in their group.

## Whizzing it

The eBay and wheely-bin activities start with visual material: ideal for whacking up on the big IWB screen for simple discussion and annotation.

# Z to A

Or A-Z if you really insist on it...

## The basic idea

Give students a topic or a theme or a text. Their task is to think of a significant key word related to that topic or text beginning with each letter of the alphabet. Individually or in any size group.

### Applying it

• Produce an A-Z for any long novel, individually, in pairs or groups, or collectively as a class. For younger students, try an A3 illustrated A-Z for *Harry Potter*, or Pullman's *His Dark Materials*, and you've wallpapered the classroom or corridor.

• Use Teachit resource **Key Stage 4/5>Media & Non-Fiction>Media & Non-Fiction Essentials>Media Terms** as a set of possible answers for an A-Z of media terminology. Try it as a revision quiz.

• Use as an 'everything we already know about {literature} {language} {poetry} {drama} {the novel}' refresher activity after the latest bout of exams seems to have wiped everything clean inside the students' heads. Good starter for AS induction.

### What's the point?

It encourages students to summarise and organise their knowledge in a constrained way. Those constraints provide something for their brains to chafe against constructively, producing pearls of lateral thinking. It can also be a useful revision tool.

### Tricks of the trade

Only use this technique with a text or topic with lots of different ideas and components to create the scope for the production of something meaningful. It's a good idea to sketch out a complete answer yourself, partly to test whether or not it'll work first (especially if you've got someone coming in to observe your lesson!), partly so that you can provide little clues for any students or groups where the chafing is getting bloody.

### Variations on a theme

• Open evening coming up? Employ your resident slave labour in producing a nice illustrated A-Z of whatever courses or key stages you're looking to promote.

• For a quicker version, or to give more support to less imaginative students, give clues for 26 key words defined by you. Try cryptic clues for stronger students, or let students choose between 'coffee time' and cryptic ones.

• To encourage divergent thinking, tell them at the start that you will give a prize for every item a group has that no-one else has got.

### Whizzing it

Have your class create an A-Z revision webpage with letter hyperlinks taking them off into different sets of notes and useful resources.

# Zimmer frames

Love 'em or loathe 'em

## The basic idea

Extended writing is difficult. Make it easier by giving students a framework or structure that supports them. Some people argue that this is reductive, with about the same level of joyful challenge as constructing a flatpack. Some people don't.

### Applying it

- For your ladies' touring bike of a zimmer frame, try straightforward structured prompts, such as those used to help murder mystery stories along in Teachit's *Key Stage 3> Genre>Murder mystery – writing>Write your own murder mystery*.

- For a chunky 4-wheel drive of a zimmer frame, outline paragraph content and sentence starters are the thing, as in Teachit's resource for Victorian ghost stories *Key Stage 4>Prose>Prose Study: Ghost Stories*.

- For the high wire unicycling AS/A2 student, Teachit's skeleton essay proforma *Key Stage 5>Skills>Essay writing>Skeletons* goes with a resource on improving conceptualised argument in advanced essay writing.

### What's the point?

Well, that's a highly contentious matter of opinion. At best, it can help students develop their extended writing skills by making the structure, content and treatment of content transparent. At worst, it becomes a mindless 'join the dots' activity that all students become dependent upon, good students become deeply bored and unchallenged by, and makes marking an almost completely pointless activity because you wrote the essay in the first place. Use it wisely and sparingly.

### Tricks of the trade

Find the line between appropriate scaffolding for some students and doing all the work for them so they don't have to think. Extended writing is a complex activity and it takes time to develop; if students never get to practise it for real, and to make whopping great mistakes from which they can learn, they will never be able to do it. Where is that line? If it takes you longer to create the frame than it does them to complete it, you've got it in the wrong place.

### Variations on a theme

- If you're working on good essay writing technique, try doing it the other way round. Give them some very good essays and get them to deduce the successful features. For extra support, give them prepared labels to apply to the relevant features. Likewise with newspaper articles or any other kind of text. Double the whammy by getting students to write instructional guides to that kind of writing.

- Make frames as minimal as you can, with just the bare bones of the structure. Get students working together to decide on relevant content prompts.

- Encourage creativity by getting students to adapt a frame rather than use it unthinkingly. Deliberately make it a bit rubbish, tell them it is, and then ask 'how could this be improved?'

### Whizzing it

Get students brainstorming initial ideas. Then whack up your frame on the IWB and explore how some of these might slot into the structure and/or re-shape.

# Zombie killers

## Keeping students alert during videos/lectures

## The basic idea

Straightforward watching of a DVD/video or listening to a radio programme or lecture can be a real struggle for some students. Help them develop valuable skills for coping with this kind of presentation, without chopping it up into bite size pieces, by giving them a more active role to play during and after the presentation.

### Applying it

• Give students responsibility for a particular kind of thinking during the presentation. Have one student in a group watching and listening with a positive thinking hat on, finding all the good things in the presentation: useful ideas, powerful lines, important information. Have another wearing the hat of critical doom, finding all the weaknesses in the presentation: logical flaws, factual errors, pointless moments. A third could be thinking of questions, and a fourth picking out the most important examples or critical moments. Afterwards, get groups together to pool ideas and information, and produce an evaluative verbal or written summary.

This is particularly good when watching documentaries, and especially if those documentaries are a little bit dated (that Story of English video you've still got in your stock cupboard). Instead of switching off because the presenter is wearing 1970s brown polyester flares, students know they are going to get the opportunity to critique it.

• Give out bingo cards with key quotations or examples or pithy bits of information. Students have to cross them off as they encounter them. Make sure it's not possible for anyone to win until very near the end.

This works well with documentaries and productions of literary texts. To go beyond the simple task of keeping them awake in a nice warm dark classroom, give them the challenge of not only crossing off the quotation but also adding a response in that square – one word responses will be fine. Then you will have a useful basis for subsequent discussion.

• If it's a lecture presentation you're giving (to help prepare AS/A2 students for higher education), plant questions in the audience. Put these on cards with different numbers, letters or symbols on them which correspond with numbers, letters or symbols interspersed through your PowerPoint slides. They have to concentrate because when their symbol appears they have to ask their question (or a different one if they prefer).

### What's the point?

It keeps students thinking actively during what can be a very passive process. You can, of course, set comprehension questions instead – these are just some ways of mixing it up a bit. The first task encourages critical thinking; this is important as there can be a tendency for students to take what appears on a TV screen as unassailable fact. The second one is more subtle than it looks. Yes, it's a cheap popular game, but at the end of the video or presentation get each student to tell you how many squares they have unmarked and you will have an instant tool for self-evaluation of listening skills. The third task is fun, but it also gets students used to asking questions in a lecture context. It doesn't matter at all to start with that you've planted them: as they get used to the format, they will start to ask their own, especially if you give them questions that are deliberately a bit lame.

### Tricks of the trade

With the first task it can be a good idea to specify a minimum number of points that students need to make, otherwise there can be a tendency for them to start brightly and then fade as the hypnotic powers of TV overtake them. Or try setting a time trial, with one point every ten minutes or something, depending on how long the presentation or programme is. With the bingo task, make sure you give students five minutes before you start to review what's on their card.

### Variations on a theme

• Mix up the types of thinking each student engages in according to the level and task. It could as easily be facts, opinions and examples; or ideas about different themes; or whatever else suits your purpose. The point is to make sure that if one student doesn't listen, s/he lets the group down in the subsequent task...

• To go one more challenge level up with the bingo task, give students in small groups the same bingo cards. Don't allow any shouting out of bingo until five minutes (maybe a bit more) after the end of the presentation or programme. In this time, they exchange their responses and discuss the significance of their quotations. Then see who wants to shout. IF they have a full house AND they can explain the significance of each quotation, then they get the glory of winning.

# Zooming in and out

Focusing on small details by getting rid of the rest

## The basic idea

Rather than trying to see the whole picture all at once, zoom in on very small pieces of detail and build ideas outwards from there. This can be particularly useful for the study of language and style in any key stage.

## Applying it

• For a sharp focus on language in a passage or a poem, strip out all the verbs, or nouns, or adjectives, or adverbs, and look at them in a decontextualised list. This can be very helpful in exploring more specific types of nouns, verbs, adjectives and adverbs. Once some ideas have been generated, review them back in context to explore their stylistic effects.

• For more general work on the language of a text, give students a specific number of words to pick out and focus on: the five most powerful words; the seven words used that are most characteristic of the writer's style; the three adjectives used that best capture a character. In group or whole class discussion, review all the choices people have made and work towards agreement of a final list of five or seven or whatever.

• Reduce the poem or passage to an alphabetical list of its constituent words. Explore what patterns and connections emerge from viewing the text like this, and/or get students writing their own poems with the words before they read the published version. Share readings and explore the mood and texture of the work produced. Use these ideas to inform readings of the text and to develop an understanding of the roles and functions of different types of words.

### What's the point?

It can help to crystallise thought through intense concentration on a smaller number of details than are more usually handled in reading a text. By taking things out of context, different kinds of clarity are possible, and some students handle this approach much better than starting with a grand overview.

### Tricks of the trade

Getting the students to pick the words is the easy bit; it's how you handle the follow through that makes the difference between students having a list of words

and them having an understanding of how the text works. Get them filtering the collective word pool so that discussion takes place, comparing ideas and putting the list back in context to see the significance. Good questioning is crucial to whole class discussion here.

### Variations on a theme

• This also works well with the five most important events in the novel; the three most important scenes or speeches in a play; and the top ten quotations in a chapter.

• For a faster or more scaffolded variation, get students to pick from a list.

### Whizzing it

Use an electronic copy of the set text and search for key patterns of imagery. To do this either drop the text into Word and use the 'find' tool, or use the online searchable texts available through the Literature Network at **http://www.online-literature.com/**. Try searching for wind, rain, dogs, windows, and doors, in *Wuthering Heights*, before exploring the significance of these patterns

Subscribers to Teachit can use 'Cruncher' to crunch texts down to word lists of different sorts: check out the **Whizzy Things** section of the site. There are instructions there as well as oven-ready word lists for creative and analytical work that you can dish straight up in your classroom.

There are also many other ready-made activities of this type on the NATE CD-ROM *Unlocking Literature*, suitable for use in the PC suite or with an IWB. This includes poems where the words have been hidden by 'bricks' and students get to uncover them bit by bit. You could start by uncovering the title, then the end word of the first line. Get students to pick which word to uncover next to see how quickly they can deduce the rhyme scheme (if it has one). Get them making predictions about the poem. Gradually zoom out until it's all uncovered.